# Fishi h

Fred J. Ta



Stanley Paul, London

Stanley Paul & Co Limited
3 Fitzroy Square, London W1P 6JD

An imprint of the Hutchinson Publishing Group

London Melbourne Sydney Auckland
Wellington Johannesburg and agencies
throughout the world

First published as *Tench* by Macdonald 1971
This edition wholly revised and enlarged
published by Stanley Paul & Co. Ltd 1979


Set in Monotype Times New Roman

Printed in Great Britain by The Anchor Press Ltd
and bound by Wm Brendon & Son Ltd,
both of Tiptree, Essex

British Library Cataloguing in Publication Data

Taylor, Frederick James
Fishing for Tench. – Completely revised and updated
ed.
1. Tench fishing
I. Title II. Tench
799.1'7'52 SH691.T4

ISBN 0 09 138690 X cased
0 09 138691 8 paper

# Contents

The line drawings are taken from originals by Ted Andrews and Peter Drennan.

# Foreword

Many years ago, Fred Taylor wrote to me, asking for information about the perch fishing at Arlesey Lake, from which we were catching at that time some very big fish of that species. The outcome was that we met at Arlesey, and I was invited to fish for tench with Fred and his brothers in the lakes at Wotton Underwood, where we had many days of great sport and good fellowship together. It took but a short time for me to realize that Fred and his brothers had little to learn about the art of catching tench, either at Wotton or on any other water that held these fish.

Not only were they thoroughly conversant with the location and behaviour of the species; they were equally well informed about effective baits, methods and tackle, and their catches were enormous, usually including good numbers of the larger specimens.

Eventually I persuaded Fred to write a book about tench fishing, and many would-be tench fishers had reason to be grateful for it. It is difficult to imagine how any angler, having read it, could fail to catch tench anywhere.

RICHARD WALKER

# 1 Thoughts on Tench and Tench Waters

My first recollection of going fishing is of being tied to a long rope which was in turn fastened to a stake driven into the ground near the River Thame. My parents lived virtually on the banks and it was possible to fish from our back garden, so I'm told. My father always had a rod made up in the shed and spent many of his spare moments fishing. To make sure that I did not fall in (because I apparently refused to be left behind) he staked me down.

Father fished mainly for roach, but there were some deep still corners where he caught tench and so I could, I suppose, claim that this was my introduction to tench fishing. If so, I have been at it a long time.

It was some years, however, before I actually hooked a tench. Again I was with my father. We were fishing at Halton reservoir in Bucks from a boat, and my two uncles accompanied us. I was using two joints of a roach pole and a tight line. The roach were feeding madly and I was one really excited boy. I had learned how to bait up with a grain of stewed wheat, how to swing the float out, and how to let the rod bend when a fish was on. I was only a small boy but I was already a fisherman.

I didn't see the bite that tench gave me; it was just on when I went to lift out the tackle, but I shall never forget it. It came thrashing to the surface and I forgot all I had been taught in my excitement. It was huge and so different from the roach I'd been catching that I wanted it in the boat at once. Of course the tackle broke and the fish was lost, but not before all three adults in the boat had seen it. They all agreed that it must have weighed over six pounds. They caught several four and five pounders that day and I am still in no doubt that my fish was much bigger than any the grown-ups took. I cried, of course, but silently so that they would not see; and I carried on with my roach fishing, but it was not the same.

It is ironical that I have never to this day, to the best of my knowledge, hooked a tench as big as that one. Perhaps I never shall, but although it was a long time before I actually landed my own first tench, my fishing was done from then on with thoughts of tench in mind. Is it any wonder?

At first I believed that all waters held tench and that the best bait for them was a grain of stewed wheat. I was to learn, however, that there were many waters which did not hold tench and that those which did differed in so many respects that methods and baits had to be altered to suit each situation.

It took a long time to realize this, and even when it began to dawn upon me at quite an early age that many of the rule-of-thumb methods passed on to me by local experts, and the basic tench-fishing formulas in the books I read, were quite unreliable. I was reluctant to change them. It is not easy to change the thinking of several generations nor is it easy to try something new while the old is still producing results.

I had always been told, and all the books said so too, that it was necessary to fish hard on the bottom for tench. The big bait had to be cast out at dawn to lie undisturbed in the groundbaited swim; and the float had to lie at half-cock. The bite, when it came, would be a series of dithers followed by a long glide-away of the float which would eventually be pulled under, out of sight. The unfortunate thing about all this was that it worked! Sooner or later, irrespective of bait, depth, tackle, or the water being fished, a tench would behave in the manner expected of it and would be caught, thus adding strength to what was really a false doctrine. The truth is, of course, that time spent waiting for the textbook tench bite could well have been exploited in other ways and the results would have been many, many more tench caught.

I was to learn all this over the years and I was to learn to some extent how and when to apply different tactics to deal with new and different situations. I could never forget the first tench I had hooked. My bait had not been big but very small. It had not been lying on the bottom but suspended a few inches off it. The bite had come at midday and it had not been a glide-away affair, for I had not seen the float move at all. It seemed to me that there was a lesson to be learned and a puzzle to be solved if only I could get down to *thinking* a bit more about tench and refrain from following blindly the doctrines preached by so many so-called experts of that era.

I fished many waters for tench. Rivers, ponds pits, canals, lakes and so on with a fair degree of success. After the war I travelled further afield and I began to appreciate subtle differences between tench waters which were outwardly very similar. Thus I began to see that there were different *types* of tench water and waters where tench behaved quite differently, because of either environment or outside influences.

There were still waters and moving waters, deep waters and shallow waters, weedy waters and weed-free waters, clear waters and muddy waters, waters with constant levels and waters which fluctuated, spring-fed waters and static waters, soft bottomed waters and hard bottomed waters, large waters and small waters, natural waters and man-made waters, over-stocked waters and well balanced waters, fertile waters and barren waters, and there were the in-betweens.

To say that each and every water needed an entirely different technique or approach would not be true, but 'basic formula' fishing would have been largely a waste of time in the great majority of them.

There were waters which simply would not respond to orthodox bottom fishing as we know it, there were waters where time of day did not seem to be important, there were waters which did not need groundbait at all, and there were waters where the tench behaved more like carp. They all had their own problems, some of which were never really solved and I doubt if they ever will be, but at least there was pleasure in trying. Common factors appeared here and there, which sometimes helped to point the way to success but which all too often led to yet another problem.

I caught tench and I am pleased to say I am still catching them. Some have been easy, some difficult; some, which I have failed so far to catch, could probably be regarded as well nigh impossible, but we shall see.

One thing has always puzzled me, for example, and that is how tench waters develop. How do waters produce big tench when 'tiddler' tench are, or appear to be, non-existent? They must be present but we seldom if ever catch them.

Of all the irritating little problems I've encountered in a lifetime's fishing, the 'tiddler' tench phenomenon has always left me guessing. I do not have any explanation whatsoever, and I suppose I am still as puzzled now as I was when I started trying to study tench fishing seriously over thirty years ago. I have had theories and I've had experiences to back them up, but nowhere along the line has it been possible for me to say 'We don't catch tiddler tench because. . . .'

Conclusions arrived at regarding the tench in one water do not apply to those in others, and I believe the mystery will remain. Even controlled experiments taken over a period of years, and involving different waters, will not provide the answers to the overall picture. But is this not true of many other situations involving other species? Findings on – say – the Shannon system in Ireland would obviously differ from those on the Grand Union Canal and so on.

No one knows this better than the scientists engaged in the research, which is why they emphasize that their findings are 'the result of experiments carried out on such-and-such a water'. In the process, however, a great deal of useful general information almost certainly comes to the fore.

I have, over the years, had many experiences involving *small* tench but I cannot claim to have found out much about *immature* or 'tiddler' tench.

My first experience came just after World War Two, on the middle lake at Claydon, presently the home of giant catfish and occasional big zander, and where I had the experiences described in Chapter 4.

The tench there were of fair quality but not super-specimens. I heard tell of bigger fish but I think perhaps the best to be hoped for was in the region of four and a half pounds.

I never saw a fish under two and a half pounds and in those days bags of up to a dozen tench were always on the cards. During the war the lake was polluted, pike of up to twelve pounds were killed off and from then on I never heard of another pike being taken from that water. In the immediate post-war years we continued to catch tench, but the average size gradually became smaller until, as I recall very vividly, one August Bank Holiday my brother Ken and I caught forty tench in a morning, ranging from two pounds down to less than two ounces. I thought then, and I still think now, that the numbers of tench increased because of the absence of pike predation. More tench fry survived and because of the reduced food supply (plus the fact that the roach and rudd population exploded) lowered their individual average weight. Future re-stocking programmes completely altered the lake's ecology and it was no longer possible to theorize. An interesting offshoot comes to the fore here, however, and while it has little to do with the topic under discussion, it is possibly worth recording.

The re-stocking included a number of big catfish and shortly after that tench became almost non-existent. I mention this because Franz Domhof of Holland once wrote that the best bait for a big Wels catfish was a three-pound tench! I have not fished the lake for many years now, but I am regularly informed of catches there and I cannot recall offhand any mention of tench.

An interesting point about the middle lake at Claydon was the complete absence of soft weed in those days. Rushes and reeds grew thick, but the rest of the lake with its mud bottom was, to all intents and purposes, devoid of soft weed.

An almost identical transformation came about at around the same time in Hartwell Lake some twenty miles away. Tench, before the war, averaged three pound; pike were taken to my certain knowledge up to twenty-one pound. A simular pollution killed them off and it became relatively easy to catch a hundred small tench in a day.

Each year the numbers appeared to increase while the individual average size became smaller. Again I put it down to the absence of pike predation and I am confident that my theory was correct with regard to that particular water. It led me to disbelieve the theory that pike do not eat tench and having since found tench inside pikes' stomachs I have no reason to think that pike are in any way diet conscious.

Now let us look at another entirely different situation, one which, to some extent, may offer a suggestion as to why we don't often catch tiny tench from big tench waters on regular baits. Wotton Lakes have been known for their big tench and big tench catches for many years. I have never caught a really small fish there, but on one occasion, when I drifted the boat over a shallow, heavily weeded area, I spotted a small shoal of tench averaging perhaps an ounce or two apiece. They were in a small pocket, completely surrounded by impenetrable weed, and I imagined they were of the same spawning. It was, I believe, August when I spotted them, but whether or not they were of that year's spawning, I have no way of knowing. I think it's highly possible.

I tried every trick I knew to catch one of those babies, just to satisfy a personal urge, but I failed. They were interested in very fine cloud groundbait and appeared to 'absorb' it as it sank, but they would have nothing to do with a single maggot or a tiny piece of paste fished on a fine link. They appeared almost incapable of

Tiddler tench. Fish of this size are seldom caught by anglers

recognizing what must have been to them a large food portion. Occasionally the disturbance of the float entering the water sent them back immediately into the thick weed where they disappeared completely for several minutes at a time. They were, I'm sure, almost completely immune from a pike in that situation and this particularly interesting episode in a lifetime's tench fishing leads me to ask some questions. Please note that I am *only* asking questions. I don't know the answers.

Do young tench, where the situation demands it, remain in the safety of thick weed until they are reasonably immune from pike? Do they only feed on microscopic life at that stage? How long does it take them to reach – say – two pounds in these circumstances? Are they thinned out by pike the following winter when much of the weed has gone and they are lying semi-torpid and vulnerable? Are their numbers thus controlled so that those remaining are able to exploit the extra food supply and put on weight quickly?

If the answer to the last question should be 'yes', it would indicate an incredible growth rate during the second year, and I wonder if there is any way of finding out just how quickly tench can convert food into body weight.

I can only speak from experience of the waters I fish, but it is a fact that all the waters I know to hold big tench also hold big pike. Whether or not you believe the 'balance of nature' theory, there does seem to be a connection, but I am not suggesting that pike are essential to good stocks of big tench. They happen to be present in the waters I fish but for all I know there may be waters where tench thrive without them.

Without knowing the history of a water it is impossible even to guess at the answers. Minor changes occur every year, of course, but these have little immediate effect upon the tench population. Drastic changes, however, appear to show results the following year.

An example of what I have in mind concerns the recent developments in the Warrells Lake at Wotton. This lower lake was the scene of many superb tench catches over a twenty-year period and I doubt if I ever saw a tench under two pounds there until recently.

Following a 'natural' pollution a few years ago, many pike, tench, roach and rudd were killed. It was a shattering experience to see so many prime fish dead, but despite what appeared to be a complete wipe-out, the water has made a remarkable recovery. The interesting outcome, however, was the appearance of small tench on opening day the following season. Tench were still present despite our worst fears and, although a few reasonable specimens were taken, most were between about a quarter and one and a half pounds. These weights were so completely different from those we'd learned to accept as normal that we had mixed feelings about the future. Were we about to witness a complete turnabout? Would the Warrells Lake now deteriorate into a 'small tench' water?

Most of us took the optimistic view and felt that the reduction in the pike population (fortunately losses were fewer than we'd thought) had allowed more small tench to survive and that this was nature's way of putting things right.

Since then a few more pike have been added to the water. Those remaining after the pollution have made a remarkable recovery, and while the average size of the tench is still below par, there is a distinct improvement. I personally took a near four pounder from the water earlier this season and I'm convinced we shall be back to normal in a season or two.

From the examples quoted it would appear that pike are part of the general picture, but I'm too long in the tooth to draw positive conclusions.

I could quote a dozen other examples of waters holding small and tiddler tench at some time or other, and none of them, to the best of my knowledge holds, or ever held, pike. But I could never be really sure. There are lots of small waters near my home holding hordes of small tench. Some appear to hold little else apart from a few tiny perch.

One, which used to hold a big head of tench running to a two pound maximum held a handful of carp. As the old carp died off the numbers of small tench increased, and it was not uncommon to see nets holding half a dozen ranging from about two ounces to half a pound. Then we introduced about eighty small carp and followed it up with twenty-three bigger fish ranging from six to fourteen pounds. Today, I firmly believe that if we drained the water completely, we'd be lucky to find a single tench. The small roach and rudd are still there in large numbers; there is, or appears to be, a big improvement in the roach generally. But I have not seen a tench there since the carp literally took over. I could go on and on.

Meanwhile modern tench fishing proceeds along lines vastly different from those used before the Second World War. The success of many of the methods now in use has been brought about by the realization that there is more to tench fishing than chucking out a bait and waiting for a fish to hang on to it! Although most waters will at some time or other respond to several different baits and methods, there are many where specialist tactics are the only ones likely to succeed. A very successful approach on one water may fail dismally on another and without knowledge of the water one can only apply trial and error tactics until the right combination is found.

The ways of catching tench are many and varied and it is my intention to try and list them all here in this book. I make no claims for having invented anything new in tench fishing, for I am sure that many other anglers have had the same ideas in the past. All I will say is that in my pursuit of tench I have discovered things for myself for the first time and that I have been able to develop ideas to deal with special situations in particular waters.

Certain waters have been the scenes of important developments in my tench fishing and other anglers with similar problems have been kind enough to write and say that my ideas have worked for them too, which pleases me.

I think, therefore, that rather than discuss the merits of the various methods here, it would be more interesting to discuss the various waters to which they apply and, where possible, to give the reasons for their application.

# 2 Early Days

## The Waterfall

The Waterfall, or 'the Lake' as we used to call it, was really an artificial cutting off the River Thame, part of an old-established estate. The water opened up into a wide lake-like mass, almost dead still apart from a narrow channel in the middle which flowed gently over a pile of rocks forming a man-made waterfall.

For the greater part of the summer it was almost completely covered with yellow waterlilies, but here and there were wide clear holes a few yards out from the shore. Weeping willows lined the banks and water mint was strong in the air in the early mornings.

The whole area was really strictly private but the keeper used to turn a blind eye on those who went along there to fish. There were no more than half a dozen holes to fish, but then there were never more than half a dozen anglers anyway. There was no competition for space, only for the best hole – or what was considered the best hole.

The Waterfall is one of the few places I can remember where tench fishing followed traditional lines. That is to say, the hole was baited with a stiffish mixture of bread and bran and a big lobworm was cast out to lie on the bottom. The float was a big one carrying three or four shots, most of which lay on the bottom too so that it was only half cocked. Bites were traditional: slow glide-aways which, provided you were not too hasty, were easy to hit.

In the early days it was impossible for me to fish there for tench simply because I could never present my bait on the bottom. My rod was a little too short and the water was a little too deep for me to manage it. So I had to be content with fishing with my bait suspended at midwater and catching only roach and small perch. I knew nothing of slider floats then.

In those days it was a great pleasure to me to cycle with my father the four or five miles involved in darkness so that we could be in position when daylight came. Father's float, a big red-topped celluloid affair, which he called the Queen Mary, would sometimes lie motionless for hours, but sooner or later it would sail away to the bite of a tench. Other anglers would come rushing up to render assistance but he would always wave them away saying 'I've hooked the fish, now it's up to me to land it or I don't deserve it!' And he would take the landing net from between his feet, push it out and draw the tench over it, slacking off the line at the precise moment when it was essential to do so. He never *taught* me how to land a fish, or at least he never *lectured* me on how to do it, but I learned it naturally by watching him.

As the other anglers stood around and looked on I made it quite plain to them, 'That's my Dad, that is!' He was the only angler I knew who caught tench regularly from the Waterfall, and while, today, I would disagree with his views on landing fish, because I believe that to share the landing of a fish is a compliment paid and a pleasure shared, I was very proud of him.

I am quite sure now that his every move was calculated and aimed at making me a real angler. He could quite easily have fixed me up with proper tench tackle, cast it for me, and made sure that I caught a tench on almost every occasion; but, of course, he very wisely did not do so. He wanted me to learn the right way and to fend for myself. He wanted my fishing to be *difficult* so that I could appreciate it more when I began to succeed by my own efforts. I'm so glad that he did!

I suppose it was when he considered that I was competent enough to try on my own that he let me have the long greenheart rod, and I believe that he purposely found himself too busy to go fishing with me the following Sunday. So I went with Desmond, another Waterfall regular of about my own age.

Desmond worked after school in a butcher's shop and he came prepared with a big tin of oxblood which had been dried off with sausage rusk. We arrived and tackled up in darkness. I chose the hole where my father had caught three tench the previous day and Desmond chose the next one along. Soon we were joined by four or five grown-ups who seemed to resent our being there, for they had nothing to say to us.

We sat seemingly for hours without a bite and I began to get impatient. I had almost decided to set the tackle shallower and catch some small roach when my float rose quite slowly in the water, toppled over flat, and without any further ado, went under! I

Old-style tench fishing

cannot explain my feelings but, praise be, I did not get over-excited. I took up the rod, struck and was into the fish.

Then the grown-ups decided to speak! They all knew what I must do and they all shouted at the same time. But I *knew* what to do and I did it! Desmond netted my fish because I wanted him to. I did not think my trembling hands were capable of holding both net and rod!

It weighed three and a half pounds exactly and it was some time before I could rebait and get the tackle out again. That fish was the first of three with a total weight of ten pounds. Desmond had two more and, being what we were, we wrapped them in wet cloths and took them home to show our folks. It seemed a long hard pull back home on my bike that lunch time, for by now it was very hot. I was hungry too, but so anxious to show off my catch that I temporarily forgot about lunch.

Father looked at the fish and said, 'Well done! Now let's revive them so you can take them back!' I was quite shattered but knew that it was no use arguing. Out came the big zinc bath, and the hose pipe from the kitchen tap was passed through the window to fill it. The tench were put in and the bath was allowed to overflow into the drain for half an hour or so until father considered the tench were fit to travel again. Then they were re-wrapped in their wet cloths and I was despatched to return them to the water. I was told I could have my lunch when I got back and once more I set out towards the Waterfall. But I must confess I cheated!

About half way along the road were some pits controlled by the local angling club and I sneaked in there on release my fish. They swam away apparently quite happily and I have no reason to believe that they were any worse off than they were in the home from whence they came. The pits held tench of very good quality and they were in fact the scene of my next few tench-fishing lessons.

## The Pits

Traditional tench-fishing methods were good up to a point in the pits. That is to say the bait was presented on the bottom and a good steady bite was awaited. Heavy groundbaiting, however, was of little use. In fact its effect was to encourage the small roach and rudd into the swim, where they became somewhat of a nuisance. Worms, generally speaking, were not good baits and I only remember one occasion when they really succeeded. But more of that later.

The bait for the pits was bread, and if possible, new bread. It was our custom to call at the bakehouse (which was open all night) and buy a small hot white loaf on our way to the pits. We pinched a cherry-sized piece on the hook and squeezed it up tightly. It was not fished as we fish bread-flake today, with tempting fluffy edges to allay suspicion, but as a hard nut too tough for the little fish to tackle. We used mostly porcupine-quill floats with one big shot pinched on the line about a foot and a half from the hook, which was usually a no. 10 roundbend to gut.

Around the float we threw half a dozen or so similar pieces of bread – no more for fear of overbaiting – and awaited results. No one caught large numbers of tench but two or three made a pleasant morning's fishing. Generally speaking it was good sense to make an early morning start, but evenings were very good too. The last hour of daylight produced many a fine tench for me after all the other anglers had departed.

It was not always possible for me to fish early mornings because of the odd hours I had to work, but I often had free time in the week from shortly after midday and as my journey home took me past the pits I often called in and stayed on till dark. That was when I began to learn about crust fishing.

I used to meet a serviceman there who was interested only in roach fishing and he fished one special pit which was noted for its quality roach.

He used floats with thin stems and cork bodies situated well down the lower half. Antenna floats, of course, but I did not know them by that name. I noticed how stable they were in the wind and how delicately they responded to biting fish. He was meticulous about his depth setting, his tackle was very fine, and his one shot was pinched on only about three inches or so from his baited hook. He was a good angler. He came from another part of the country where techniques had developed somewhat differently, but he was applying his skill and knowledge extremely well. I found myself becoming more and more interested in his particular style and began to practise it myself.

As dusk began to fall the roach would feed and I became quite adept. I lost one or two good fish, which I fondly imagined were outsize roach but which I was to learn later were tench. It never occurred to me, until I had one kicking on the bank, that this method would catch tench too. But of course it did, and it was but a short step then to what is now called the lift method, as we shall see. Already there was a noticeable difference in bites. There was no waiting for these crust bites; they had to be hit very quickly and a different style of tench fishing was already becoming apparent to me. Its application was to be of great use in years to come but meanwhile other ideas began to form.

In one of the bigger pits a big billowing cloud of soft silkweed came up from the bottom, ending about four or five feet from the surface and being several feet thick. When the sun shone it showed up green and lush and tench could sometimes be seen swimming lazily over it. They were seemingly quite uncatchable in this particular situation. All attempts to lay a bait where it could be seen were defeated because it immediately sank into complete obscurity in the weeds. Baits presented so that they hung suspended from a float directly above the weed were ignored, probably because they were so obviously unnatural.

We believed, in those days, too, that fish you could see could not be caught anyway, and that this was just a case in point.

Joe Taylor, however, got to grips with them one hot August bank holiday. He watched their movements from a vantage point behind a bush and while doing so he fed them loose pieces of bread flake. He found that by pinching only part of it up tightly the whole piece would sink very slowly and settle on the weed.

Bread pulled from the crumb of a loaf will float as a rule. Pinch it up tightly and it will sink like a stone. But pinch it lightly in the middle and there will be just enough weight applied to overcome the natural buoyancy of the crumb. Furthermore, if a piece of new flake is flattened so that it becomes a thin disc it, too, will sink slowly and with a swinging motion until it settles lightly. Joe tried these things and eventually saw a tench pick up one of his free offerings. From then on it was a simple matter to remove the shots from his line and pinch a suitably treated piece of flake on his hook. He left his float on, of course. In those days we could not visualize the possibility of fishing without one!

I'm not sure of the count now but I believe Joe took five tench in the middle of the afternoon on that hot summer's day. How many lessons can be learned from that little episode? And how far removed are we now from traditional tench-fishing lore?

Apart from the bait presentation, which becomes more and more important as tench fishing becomes more and more involved, the vital thing about it was the proof that tench could be caught at the time of day and in conditions which were both regarded as totally unsuitable. It could be done and what is more, like justice, it could be seen to be done!

For many years there has been a supposed association between tench and tar. Somewhere, back in the files of angling history, someone suggested that lobworms dipped in tar were excellent tench baits and this advice has been repeated from time to time even up to the present day. Frankly I have never tried dipping my worms in tar and, having struggled to acquire and store a supply, I would be reluctant to kill them off (as this would surely be the outcome) by dunking them in some foul-smelling concoction.

A range of modern floats – vastly different from those cork and quill types used for early tench fishing

I once had an interesting experience with tarred worms, however, and as the incident occurred at the pits where worms were regarded as very poor tench baits, it may be worth recording here.

It had rained very heavily overnight and the morning was warm and overcast as my father and I made our way to the pits. The road had been freshly tarred and sanded and we were surprised to see large numbers of worms stretched out on it. Obviously they had come out with the rain and had become marooned in the sand and tar. They were half-dead, sorry looking creatures, but we picked some of them up. Father said 'Lobworms and tar for tench. Now we'll be able to find out.' And find out we did! For a brief period the tench in the pits fed madly and we compiled a good catch before going home to a very late breakfast.

Are lobworms dipped in tar good tench baits? I don't know. I've never tried them since. It was certainly an unusual catch for the pits, but I'm not so sure that the tar made any difference. I have a feeling that good clean lobworms would have succeeded just as well on that particular morning!

The pits were the scene of many of my angling 'firsts' and I shall always remember their fairyland atmosphere; the wonderful feeling of being completely isolated although they were only a few yards off the main road to Oxford. I recall my first pike, my first big rudd, my first newt, my first sight of a fox and my first ducking. But mostly I remember my tench 'firsts'. Like the tench I caught on blood worms when I left my bait at home and the tench I caught on a wasp grub when I was fishing for roach in the manner prescribed by that great angler, the late J. H. R. Bazley.

This latter fish I actually saw taking the bait. It appeared from nowhere, dispersed the roach I had been catching and took the bait while it was on the move, sinking slowly below my small self-cocking float. I remembered it, as I remembered so many other incidents, when I was later engaged in a serious study of tench and what made them tick.

The pits, alas, are no longer there. They were used as refuse tips shortly after the Second World War. It was distressing to see them become stinking, rat-infested holes and to watch so many beautiful fish die slow and lingering deaths among the indescribable filth. Today, as I walk by the tall hedge which once hid the ghastly eyesore, I wonder why such things are still allowed to happen in a country so desperately short of fish-holding water.

## The Lake

On the other side of the road from the pits lies a fine country estate and in the middle of it is a lake. It is not a very big lake but it is very fertile and holds lots of fish. When I first fished it, it held large pike as well as tench, perch and roach. Apart from a few clear and very shallow holes here and there, the margins were completely overgrown with dense soft weedbeds. They were comprised mostly of milfoil and hornwort if I remember correctly, and although I know now that all this weed was probably very important in the lake's structure and the general scheme of things, it only meant one thing to me then. I had to learn to cast a longish way to get clear fishable water! I began to learn the importance of correctly balanced tackle and how to use the overhead cast accurately and effectively with the tackle available to me at the time. All in all I did quite well, but I must admit I caught more eels and small perch than tench.

Every so often a tench would come along, however, and then it was largely a question of whether I could haul it through the soft weed without breaking. It was all a bit of a compromise really. I needed a light line and a heavy float to achieve the distance and a fairly strong line to land the weeded fish. It was the sort of situation which taught me to think for myself and to use bigger hooks to stronger links when conditions demanded it. It made sense to me and yet I saw anglers broken time and time again because they could not adapt to conditions.

I was walking very quietly along the bank at daybreak one morning (even in those days I had learned the importance of a stealthy approach) when I saw a tench in one of the clear shallow holes in the weed. It was a very big one. Believing now, because of my pit experiences, that tench which could be seen could be caught, I crept up to it and dropped my hook, baited with a small worm, in front of its nose. Without appearing to move, the tench drifted over to it, up-ended and sucked it in. Then spat it out again very quickly! I was fascinated at the speed with which it all happened and I was considering removing the tackle when it did the same thing all over again!

I must have stayed with that tench over an hour watching it occasionally pick up and spit out my bait. I wanted that fish but I dared not strike until it took the bait properly: and finally it did. By this time, however, I was so tense and excited that I struck too hard and broke my top joint! I stayed with the fish for a few seconds longer trying desperately to handle it on my broken rod, but eventually it weeded and broke off.

Do you see now, however, the new developments in thought that this episode was bound to bring to me eventually? On two occasions at the pits I had been able to *see* tench take baits; once from the top of a cloud of silkweed, and once from mid-water while it was still sinking. But here I had seen a tench pick up a bait from the bottom; and what a ritual there had been before it finally took it properly! The bait had been in its mouth a dozen times, but the float had never moved! Many years later I was to write 'I believe baits are inside tench's mouths more often than we realize and that each time this happens it constitutes a bite which should be struck'.

I saw this sort of thing happen many times later on other waters, but never again at the lake.

There came a pollution which killed off all the pike and many other fish, but the tench survived. From then on, however, they increased in numbers rapidly and became small and stunted. When anyone asks me what was the greatest number of tench I ever caught at a sitting I can tell them truthfully that it was eighty. They came from the lake and the biggest fish weighed, possibly, a pound and a half. I stopped at eighty but I could have quite easily made it 'a ton' if I'd not become bored!

After a time I stopped fishing there altogether because I realized that my chances of a good fish were precisely nil! A small handful of groundbait brought fish swarming to the spot. The whole area 'boiled' with bubbles from small tench and the hook bait was taken within seconds of reaching the bottom.

It was possible, on some occasions, to catch an odd two-pounder by groundbaiting a spot and fishing somewhere else! The groundbait attracted the hordes of small fish away from the hook-bait and every so often it would remain there long enough for one of the slightly better tench to find it. But tench fishing such as we look forward to each summer ceased to exist once the pike had gone.

Please note that I am simply stating a fact and not suggesting that pike are necessary to ensure good quality tench! It is highly probable that the perch, which were killed off too, had helped keep the tench fry down to a tolerable level in the past. One can only speculate as to the reason, but one cannot deny the facts.

Because of this particular situation, and because I felt that I could learn no more about tench fishing from that water I looked around for somewhere else to fish and I began to concentrate, with my brother Ken, on the water where I had hooked my first tench – Halton Reservoir. Now, however, because the circumstances had changed, we fished it from the bank and not from the boat as previously.

# 3 The Reservoir

Immediately after the war fishing tackle was not always easy to obtain and it was some time before nylon monofilament became available. I was fortunate, however, in that I was given two twenty-five yard lengths of English nylon by someone I met in Lancashire who was engaged in the development of this material. While others were still using silk lines I was one step ahead with my modern material. It was then possible to buy gut substitute and also yard and two-yard casts of nylon monofil, but it was some time before it became available in hundred-yard lengths.

For some time I had fished a lot in Lancashire, mostly for roach and bream. I had caught no tench in that county, but I had learned a little about tackle. For instance I had seen fly hooks on sale in all sizes with turned-up or turned-down eyes. With monofilament it was possible to tie them directly to the cast – or even to the reel line if necessary. I thought to myself at the time that if these hooks were good enough for trout anglers they ought to be good enough for a tench angler and the next time I visited Lancashire I brought a supply home with me. No, I could not buy them in my home town – probably because there was no fly fishing.

I had also seen an angler using a piece of peacock quill attached at the bottom end only as a roach float in a small lake in the Fylde district. He wasn't using it very well as it happened because his bait was suspended at mid-water. Nevertheless, peacock quills were cheap: each one, costing a penny, made four or five floats. The eyed hooks were less than a penny each and perfectly adequate, I thought, for my type of fishing. I first put them to use on the reservoir and began to appreciate the finer points about catching bottom-feeding fish in still water.

The roach fishing was superb in those days and it was not unusual to catch fifty or sixty fish at a sitting. It was too good to miss and my brother Ken and I used to take two rods with us so that we could (as we fondly imagined) enjoy the best of both worlds. We baited the tench rods with lobworms and let them fish for themselves while we concentrated on roach fishing with the other.

Every so often, but less than once per visit, the float on the worm outfit would glide slowly away and the result would be a tench somewhere in the region of four pounds. Meanwhile, around the roach float, there would be signs of continued activity. To keep the roach going, groundbait was introduced continually, little and often. Bubbles rose to the surface, the float dithered a lot, and although we caught plenty of roach it soon became obvious that tench were interested too. There came times when all roach bites stopped and yet the water surface in the float area was a mass of tiny bubbles. Many, many times we wound in to find that our baits had been taken without our having seen a bite.

The bait we used mostly on the roach outfits was breadcrust, but we tried wheat and soft paste with reasonable results. There seemed to be no doubt about it eventually. The roach were biting much more boldly than the tench. We could see and hit the roach bites when they came, but the tench were giving no registration at all.

I thought, perhaps, that the simple answer would be to use a piece of groundbait on the hook. After all, it was the groundbait which was attracting the tench and it seemed fairly obvious that they were eating it. So for the next few visits I made up some bread and bran paste and let it lie in the groundbait area.

The float twitched and dithered continually but I can only recall one occasion when it sailed away to the confident bite of a tench. Of course, when it *did* happen I thought that, perhaps, we had found the answer. But we had not. For the greater part of the time we were driven frantic by 'bites' which did not develop and by a never-ending display of the tench's ability to strip hooks bare. In truth we never really knew whether it was just the intense activity of the tench in hook-bait area which caused the float to perform as it did, or whether in fact, they were actually whittling away at the baits continually.

The up-ending and tail-wagging movements performed by an active tench are considerable – so much so that the disturbance can actually cause the float to move along the surface of the water. This fanning action is described by Richard Walker in *Still Water Angling:*

Everyone who has fished regularly for tench must be familiar with those occasions when the fish appear to be playing with the bait and refusing to take it properly. Nearly every book on coarse fishing describes how the float will bob and dip, travelling round the swim in a maddening way, and never giving a decisive signal for the angler to strike. Various means of combating this have been suggested. One way that often works is to draw the bait slowly away from the fish, which is then supposed to grab it quickly for fear of losing what, when it was to be had too easily, it did not want. I think this presupposes a degree of perversity beyond any fish; but the fact remains that the idea does work on occasions, and the real reason for this may be due to an effect which I will describe later.

Another remedy which sometimes works is to change to finer gut and a smaller hook and bait. This is supposed to allay the suspicions aroused by stouter tackle; what happens in reality may often be quite different.

Before going any further, I must explain that I don't claim to have solved completely the problem of 'niggling' and indecisive tench bites. Tench sometimes do play about with a bait and refuse to take it properly. But it is just as often the fault of the angler, who is fishing so that the hungry tench, eager and willing to swallow the bait offered, find great difficulty in getting it into their mouths or even touching it; it is these frustrated approaches that make the float behave in that curious way ascribed by the watching angler to the tench 'playing with the bait'.

Failure to understand the behaviour of fish when they are feeding is the cause of much disappointment in angling. Anyone who has seen tench feeding on the bottom should have realized why the float so often bobs, dips, moves sideways – does anything but give decisive slanting-downwards movement that almost always precedes the solid hooking of a fish. A tench feeding in earnest stands almost vertically on its head; 'head to hell and tail to heaven', as a sporting parson once described it to me. In order to maintain this attitude, the fish 'fans' vigorously with its fins and specially with the tail.

Now consider what happens when a tench attempts to take a bait offered on the usual float tackle with a few shot on the bottom and the line or cast running almost vertically upwards to the float.

If the bait is fairly close to the shot, either because the hook-length is short or because there is a loop or coil or two between bait and shot which the angler has failed to draw straight, the tench may very likely brush against the line running up to the float. This may or may not alarm the fish; it will certainly result in movements of the float, though the bait has not been touched. Suppose the tench has not been alarmed: it waggles its tail to push its head down to the bait. The eddies thus caused wash the line sideways, the shot and bait are pulled along the bottom, and the float moves to accommodate itself to the new position of the shot. The fish finds the bait is no longer where he thought it was; rises a little from the bottom, spots it, and tries again with a similar result. A really hungry and persistent tench will keep this up for fifteen minutes or more, chasing the bait (followed by the float) all round the pitch; while the angler on the bank says to his friend, 'The tench are not hungry this morning – they're only playing with the bait.'

It may surprise many people that the water movements set up by the waggling of a tench's tail are sufficient to move the bait and shot along the bottom. But it is so. A tench a yard from the line can cause enough 'wash' to drag two or three shot; while at closer ranges, a drilled bullet weighing as much as a quarter of an ounce can be moved! I have seen it done.

Now let us return to our angler who had complained about the tench not being hungry. After a time he remembers the advice about drawing the bait away, and tries it. This lowers the angle which his line, between float and shot, makes with the bottom. It draws the gut between shot and bait perfectly straight; and it ensures that the hungry tench that has been vainly chasing the bait, now approaches it from a point directly opposite to where the shot are lying, and as far away from the line rising to the float as it can ever get. This gives the fish the best chance to get hold of the bait without washing it away from itself, and very often it succeeds.

But perhaps our imaginary angler, instead of trying the trick of drawing away the bait a little, decides to try a smaller hook and finer gut. In this case, the reasons for the occasional success of such a change are less obvious. But when tackle is changed, the changes are sometimes greater than intended. They may mean that the shots are now farther from the hook; that the depth, or rather the distance between float and shot, has been increased; quite a lot of things may be altered which, if they all minimize the 'washing-away' effect, may result in an odd fish or two being captured.

Having described the process, what is the remedy for the trouble? At the very least, two feet between bait and shot; plenty of room between shot and float, so that the line leaves the bottom not too near to the vertical; shot drawn back to ensure that the gut between it and the hook is straight, and, if necessary, the use of a drilled bullet or pear-lead to anchor everything firmly against 'washing-away' by the tails of the tench.

When tench are behaving in the manner Richard Walker describes, his subsequent alteration of the tackle presentation is undoubtedly the answer. But we also have to consider the situation when tench are not only fanning the bait along the bottom but are also sucking in and spitting out the bait very quickly.

This straightening of the tackle deals with the problem of fanning, but it also allows the tench to pick up the bait without moving the float. If, after picking up the bait, the tench swims off with it, all well and good, but if it ejects it immediately, something further has to be done. We have to remember also that crust is particularly soft in the water and that it doesn't take much to remove it from the hook completely.

Straightening out a long link tackle means that, although the line hangs perpendicularly from the float, it is too far away from the bait to be affected by the fanning. However, because of the distance between the shot and the bait, considerable movement is necessary before the float will register the bite.

What is needed is a tackle rig which will cause the float to react immediately the bait is sucked in, and, of course, it must be presented in such a way as to be unaffected by this fanning action.

Remembering the rig used by the roach angler at the pits I tried placing my shot a lot nearer to the hook. This, I thought, would give me quicker registration on the float. By setting the float a bit deeper than the water I found that the line had to be *tightened* before the float would cock. This meant that the line under the water did not rise vertically to the float but at a much less acute angle. With all tightened up the float remained steady and, because of the angle of the line, it was less affected by the fanning activity of the tench. Furthermore the setting was such that it was never necessary for the float to be pulled *under*. The moment the shot was dislodged from the bottom the float would rise up in the water and lie flat on the surface. The very powerful suction caused by a tench taking in the bait was sufficient to dislodge the shot which was pinched on so close to it.

To begin with we used pieces of peacock quill about six inches long and one big swan shot about three inches from the hook, but we later found it could be an advantage in some conditions to scale everything down to about half that size. Sometimes we fished with two inches of quill and one AA shot pinched on no more than an inch from the hook.

By this time, of course, we were beginning to appreciate the actions of different rods and were using twelve footers with tonkin butts and middles and full length built cane tops. Our rods had to do for roach, bream *and* tench, so they were fairly fast but with action through to the butt.

The lift method, as we began to call it, became our basic tench-fishing rig. We soon learned that it was essential to place the rod in a rest after the line was tightened up and to *leave* it there. We fell into the trap of picking up the rod in readiness to strike at the first sign of a 'touch' many times in the beginning, but we found that it

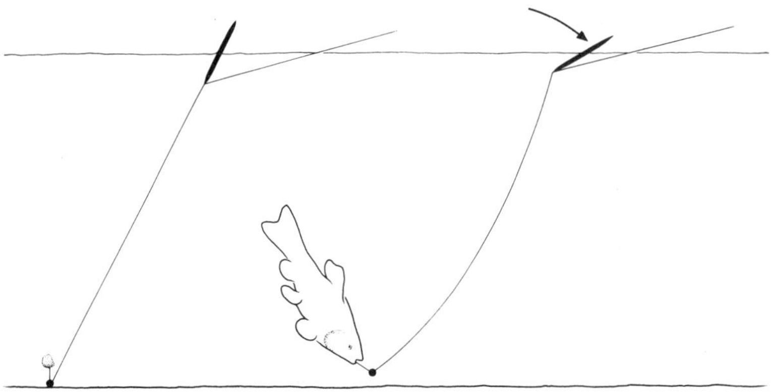

*Figure 1* The lift method

was fatal to do so. The moment the rod was taken up, the float keeled over and the rig became ineffective. We had to discipline ourselves to pick up the rod and strike in one continuous movement. We had to practise, practise, practise, but we were soon able to do it blindfold or without taking our eyes off the float. At times one of us would be otherwise occupied and looking somewhere else when the other would simply say 'strike!' Without looking or checking we grabbed the rod, struck and caught many fish by word of command!

Our baits were mostly crust, for we found that this accounted for most of our roach and tench, but occasionally we would use the same rig for worms and knobs of paste. We moved our shots farther away from the hook then, of course, because these big baits did not have to be struck so quickly.

Even then, with the delicate rig now helping tremendously with our catches, we still had a lot to learn about the finer points of lift method fishing. We really got down to it properly several years later when we began to fish Wotton Lakes, as we shall see, but before going any further let me make one thing quite clear. The lift method has been described as my idea or invention. It is not! I first saw it used wrongly and adapted it for tench fishing – but others were using it, too, well before me. The late Ted Ensom ('Faddist') mentioned it in his book on roach fishing a long time before I began to use it. He called it the 'shot leger'. I can only claim to have used it, studied it, developed it a little and probably made it more popular for tench fishing than it ever was before. It was Joe Taylor, I believe,

An early 'lift method' tench

who first called it the lift method, but whoever it was, one or other of us can rightly claim to have given it a name which has stuck.

The reservoir is different now. It is used for boating and so-called sailing (though most of the sailors I have seen there seem to spend their time becalmed and praying for a wind) and the tench fishing is poor. The methods I described would not catch many tench there today; in fact only a very few are recorded each season now. But in the early years after the Second World War the lift method worked and I felt confident that it would work on any water holding tench.

I was to learn differently as time passed. Just about then I was invited to join a couple of friends at the middle lake, Claydon, a water noted for its tench fishing at that time.

# 4 The Middle Lake

There were only two buses a week to the middle lake, and when I first began to fish it I had to be content with arriving at ten-thirty in the morning and leaving long before dark. Fortunately it was a water which responded to daytime tactics and tench catches were not dependent on early morning sessions.

It is a long narrow lake, presently controlled by Leighton Buzzard Angling Club and by no means the tench water it used to be, largely because of circumstances in no wise connected with that fine club.

When I joined my friends on the first visit, I spent much time walking around, plumbing the depth and looking for signs of tench, but I found little to encourage me. It seemed that the middle lake was just about a uniform three and a half feet deep all over. It was fed by an upper lake and it overflowed into a lower one. Both the upper and the lower lakes had more character, more plant life, more variation in depth and more outward signs of life, but those who knew the water said that it was the middle lake which held the fish. I searched hard for a small patch of weed but apart from some fairly thick marginal rushes there was very little in the way of plant life at all. Here and there the rushes had been cut back to open up swims, but the water was obviously not heavily fished at that time.

The bottom was of thick mud. In fact, I have never fished a water with a greater depth of foul-smelling, thick, black mud! From the very outset, although my two companions assured me that big lobworms were the bait supreme, I was quite convinced that they would lie for the greater part of the time buried below the surface of that mud unseen and undiscovered. I felt quite sure that crust fished on a lift rig would be much better and I determined to fish with it. It didn't take me long to find out why the others preferred worms. The middle lake was a teeming mass of tiny rudd and roach. Every bait, except big lobworms, was tackled the moment it hit the water and the float was never allowed to cock before the bait was gone.

Worm baits may have been tweaked on their way to the bottom, but once they had settled the small fish no longer touched them. The reason seemed obvious to me. The worms were sinking out of sight in the mud and were remaining there untouched because the small roach and rudd were not prepared to 'dig' for them.

Tench, on the other hand, were, and it was not long before we had two or three in the net. None of them was big. A three pounder from the middle lake was a good fish (although I once caught a four pounder and rolled over an even bigger one on the same day) and ours were just about that weight.

It seemed strange at first to see the teeming hordes of small fish attack the groundbait the moment it hit the water and keep on attacking it as it lay on the bottom until it was all gone. Once it was gone, all activity in the area ceased, and the small fish moved elsewhere only to come haring back the moment a fresh ball of groundbait was introduced.

I was quite convinced that the only purpose my groundbait was serving was to feed the small fish! It was not attracting the tench, I was sure.

I thought, perhaps, that it might be advisable to use the groundbait to attract the small fish *away* from my tench bait. I figured that a tench would not be likely to find a single lobworm in the mud beneath all that commotion. Besides which, I thought, it might give me a chance to fish with some bait other than lobworms, and accordingly I scattered some loose dry sausage rusk over the surface of the water. It drifted away gradually in the breeze and I supplemented it with several crusts of bread, which drifted away too. The small fish followed and my swim quietened. I fished with paste, crust, flake and maggots, but I had no bites either from small fish or from tench. Undoubtedly my ruse was successful in enticing away the unwanted small fish but it did not serve any useful purpose in helping me to catch tench.

My two friends, although continually bothered by small fish, caught a few more tench in their baited swims. I caught nothing, and it began to appear as if they were right about the lobworms and that the traditional approach was the best one for the middle lake.

It is not possible to learn much in a short day's fishing, however, and I was impressed enough by the water to want to return and learn some more. I fished it regularly from then on and applied all my newly gained knowledge with very little effect. By this I mean I fished early and late and employed all the little tricks I had learned, but in truth I only really caught tench when I was fishing with lobworms lying on the bottom. An uncle of mine had told me that worms would be less likely to bury in the mud if their heads had been nipped off and so I tried 'tail ends' with, I believe, slightly better results. This was probably coincidence and the more I think about it the more I am inclined to believe it was.

I enjoyed my tench fishing and I caught my fair share of fish, but I was convinced that there ought to be ways and means of catching them more regularly.

I don't know what made me try my new tactics; it was probably because I became very bored waiting for the float to glide away in the manner I had got to know so well.

I decided one morning to see just how many small rudd and roach I could catch. I wondered if they would keep feeding at the same astonishing rate all day if I kept catching them and putting them in a keep net. I wondered too, if the effect of actually *removing* some of them from the water would in any way affect the behaviour of the tench.

I made up a second rod, a Spanish reed twelve footer with a tip action, and I set to work on those tiddlers with a vengeance. I used a no. 14 hook tied to 3 lb breaking-strain nylon and a small piece of quill cocked by one AA shot. My groundbait was a fine cloud mixture aimed at attracting, but not really feeding, the small fish.

To begin with it was ridiculous! I only had to drop in and lift out and there was a small rudd attached. I caught ninety of them in the first half hour and if you find that hard to believe, I assure you that a rate of three per minute was easy to maintain. A really good match angler would have doubled it!

After a while, however, things quietened down and bites came less frequently. It was noticeable that more groundbait was needed to keep the bites coming and I finally settled down to a steady rhythm of casting, baiting and fish-catching. My worm on the other outfit meanwhile remained untouched.

Then came a bite – no different from all the rest which I struck in the normal way but which nearly pulled me off the old wooden sleeper on which I was precariously balanced. It was as if I had hit a brick wall, but a brick wall which suddenly decided to move away from me at a remarkable speed!

I was taken completely by surprise, but managed to recover

sufficiently to tackle the situation. It was a tench I had hooked, of course, and although the rod I was using was really hopelessly inadequate for that particular task I managed to control and land it. Fortunately there were no weeds or snags and I was able to let the fish go where it wanted to until it tired. That was one of my most exciting tench captures.

The fish weighed just three and a half pounds and on the tackle I was using took about four minutes to subdue, but this was only part of the excitement. All the time I was playing with it I was wondering if this was just an accident, a tench which just happened to come along at the right moment, or if I had stumbled on a new method of catching tench from the middle lake.

I ought really to have changed tackle and continued fishing with something more adequate, but I stuck with the Spanish reed outfit for the time being and continued with my 'tiddler snatching' session. A few more small rudd and once again another 'brick wall' and another few minutes of excitement.

I shall never forget that day but I will not bore the reader with a full account of it. Suffice it to say that while my traditional tench outfit remained unmoved, my 'tiddler' rig accounted for nine tench; by far and away the most tench I had ever caught in one session up till then.

From then on, of course, I used a rod more suited to the job, but I continued to apply these tactics every time I fished the middle lake. I do not believe there is a harder form of tench fishing! It is a case of go, go, go the whole time and success really depends on keeping the small fish continually active.

Undoubtedly the small fish, or the activity of the small fish, attracts the tench, and these tactics are similar to those employed by carp anglers who use floating crusts to attract small fish in the first instance. It is a kind of *indirect* groundbaiting, a very busy form of fishing and one requiring a lot of groundbait, but a very practical one on many waters. I have since tried this approach on a number of waters with considerable success, but I am convinced that it will only work really well in waters holding large numbers of small fish.

Every time I fished I found it necessary to work like fury at the outset to remove as many small fish as possible. Only when the bites began to come much less frequently did I expect to catch tench. I found it was advisable *not* to relax for lunch or snacks because this only resulted in a build up of the small fish and another hard session of catching them before the situation improved.

A normal day's supply of groundbait for two anglers

I learned that, although groundbait was really essential to real success with the tench in the middle lake, it was possible to improvise on occasions and make do with substitutes.

On one occasion, because I shared my usual bag of groundbait with my father, we ran out about mid-afternoon. It was quite obvious that we were going to catch no more tench without first stimulating the small fish into some sort of activity so I decided to try using mud to see if the cloud effect would do the trick.

I went to the marshy area between the middle and the lower lake and began gathering some light coloured mushy clay. On my travels I came across a broken down hollow tree, the bowl of which was simply soft wood pulp. I pulled some out with my hands, and rubbing it between my fingers made it into a powder. I filled my groundbait sack, added a little of the clay and soaked it all into a soft mash. It worked perfectly. It sank slowly, formed a cloud and attracted the small fish like magic. Its effect was by no means long lasting but it resulted in our catching several more tench before we caught our bus home.

Throughout the years I fished the middle lake I had many wonderful catches. I confess now to being perhaps a bit of a know-all in those days! I have watched other young anglers develop the same complex only to learn, as I did, that it is only when you realize that you *don't* know much, that you're on the road to becoming a reasonably competent angler!

On the other hand, it was perhaps excusable. I was catching a lot more tench than anyone else who fished the water in those days, and I made no bones about saying so! It irritated me to hear anglers, much older and with much more experience, telling me that I was fishing all wrong and that my tactics only attracted small fish, when by the end of the day my catches were often four to five times as great as theirs! It irritated me, too, when after walking round to ask me what I was using, and how, they told me they weren't prepared to go to such lengths to catch tench! I could not understand this attitude. Perhaps I was intolerant, but why ask if the advice is not going to be heeded?

Throughout my fishing life I have always listened and tried the methods and tactics advised by local anglers with experience of the waters concerned. Very often, perhaps more often than not, I have developed *away* from their general practices and found something more suitable, but I have always been prepared to listen and follow the advice given to me by those who *caught fish*! I shall always do so.

I did not learn a great deal more about the tench in the middle lake after that. The best catch I ever had there was twenty-one fish on a very hot day when I fished from dawn to dusk. The fish on that day averaged a lot smaller than usual and it was not many years before the whole balance of the lake altered. The tench and small rudd seemed to disappear completely following re-stocking programmes, and roach and bream have dominated the scene in turn since those days. At the time of writing I hear that there are signs of a return of tench once more. I hope it is true! Meanwhile it serves to illustrate yet one more example of a water where tench could be caught reasonably well by traditional baits and methods, but where a slightly unorthodox approach would account for many more.

# 5 The Warrells

When the fishing at Wotton Lakes became available locally it was necessary, because of the rent involved, to form a new club of some eighty members to cope with the situation. My brother Ken and I joined.

Wotton Lakes were part of a large estate which, over the years, had been allowed to deteriorate and become overgrown. Not that this was a bad thing as far as local anglers were concerned. During the days when it was maintained by numerous gamekeepers, water bailiffs, gardeners and other staff, it was almost an offence to be caught looking over any one of the many gates shutting off the neatly trimmed and well kept drives!

In the days between the two wars the local angling club and a local works club were allowed the privilege of fishing there two days each per year, one in summer and one in winter. The number of anglers was strictly limited and there were always more applications than coach seats. Some, who were well informed regarding dates and who were members of both clubs, managed to fish on all four occasions! Such was the lure of Wotton Lakes fishing that money often changed hands between the keen without permits and the not-so-keen with them!

It was the custom in those days to fish the farther Warrells Lake during the morning, to retire to the nearby hostelry, 'The Crooked Billet', at lunchtime, and to return and fish for the remainder of the day at the nearer and larger Sawmills Lake. The Warrells was noted for its tench and fished well in the early mornings. The Sawmills, supposedly, contained no tench but produced wonderful roach and rudd during the afternoons and evenings.

My father had been on many of these trips and knew the water as well as anyone with such limited opportunities could, and when Ken and I told him of the new club, he told us a lot about the water, which we had not seen at that time.

It was 1950 and the close season. The days until 16 June seemed never ending and Ken and I looked over the water for the first time during early May. What we saw made us as impatient as only two fanatical tench anglers could be! Almost every yard of the margins seemed to be overgrown with reed and rush, but every small gap seemed to indicate a tench swim. Obviously work would have to be done before all the members could fish and Ken and I decided there and then that we would be the first to fish on opening day and that our swim would be chosen and cleared well in advance.

Being undecided where to fish we asked Dad's advice. He told us to choose the Warrells Lake and to fish, if possible, by the second summerhouse. There, he told us, he had caught many tench over four pounds and that the only trouble lay in getting the bait down past the rudd which took anything and everything offered before it could reach the bottom.

So we reconnoitred the Warrells Lake and decided to drag, cut and clean the corner by the second summerhouse in early June.

We found the lake to be roughly pear-shaped and, perhaps, ten acres or so in extent. The narrow or 'stalk' end was shallow, weedy, and very muddy. Reeds had encroached over much of the shallows and a great part of it was completely unfishable. At the wide end of the lake there was a dam, an overflow and a really dense bed of reed mace. The water a few feet out from the dam, however, was about five feet deep and plumbing the depth accurately showed that there was a narrow channel some seven or eight feet deep fifteen yards out. At each corner stood a summerhouse, a slate-roofed open shelter resting on shaped oak pillars with a central dividing wall of lath and plaster. One side of the wall faced the lake; the other faced the big house at the top of the hill. They were both obviously built to provide shelter for residents and guests when taking tea by the lake. The dividing walls took into account the changing winds and shelter was assured in all weather conditions in one or other side of either summerhouse. The second summerhouse was so called simply because it was the second one reached when walking round from the only available entrance via the larger Sawmills Lake.

Large elms and oaks overhung the lake on both sides and the area was well wooded. Only the dam end and the opposite narrow neck were grassland.

Modern day-fishing at Wotton

Looking out from the swim at the second summerhouse corner we could see most of the lake. Both sides were banked by tall reed mace which extended several lengths out. By sitting together in the middle of the area of cleared bank, Ken and I felt we could each fish comfortably in the clear water close in, or off the bank of soft weed farther out, or off the point of the reed beds which bordered our swim. Once the swim was cleared we would have a choice of depths, depending on the angle and length of our cast, from some four and a half to seven feet. All this we had planned and noted long before the season opened. So we cut and we dragged. We pulled reed mace out by the roots. We fell in and we went in intentionally to make sure that we had a clear swim and by 15 June we were satisfied. Tomorrow would be the day!

Our groundbait of bread and bran was mixed. Our worms had been gathered and tinned ready for the following morning. Our maggots had been purchased. Our bread paste had been made. Our new loaves had been wrapped in moist cloth so that we could use flake or crust if necessary. We had stewed a small pan of wheat. Our sandwiches were cut; our flasks and small spirit stoves were ready to be packed. Our rods had been overhauled. Our lines were new and our reel spools were full. We were ready to fish and it was only seven o'clock in the evening!

I knew I should never sleep and I knew that Ken felt that way too. I don't know who suggested it, but we finally decided that it would be better to go, there and then, and to settle in the second summerhouse overnight so that we could start with the following dawn. I believe we were both secretly afraid that someone would beat us to our cleared and prepared swim if we left it too late. There was little chance of either of us oversleeping, but the fear was there in our hearts!

So we packed our gear on Ken's motor cycle, put on a large overcoat each and journeyed to the Warrells.

It was a very hot evening and by the time we had made the long trek to the swim, wearing heavy coats and carrying an enormous load of gear, bait and groundbait, we were physically exhausted. We were to be glad of our overcoats later on, however, for the night turned out to be very cold.

We spent the first hour or so collecting as many dried reeds as

An early Warrells tench

we could to pile up on the stone floor of the summerhouse so as to make a reasonably comfortable bed. Then we tackled up, put our rods in rests in the swim (thus 'booking' our places), made some tea and settled down to a restless, cold and seemingly never-ending night!

We had intended to bait the swim overnight but at two a.m. we realized that we had completely forgotten to do so and decided to leave it until morning.

I remember well the first fish I caught from the second summerhouse swim and I remember the time I caught it. It was 3.25 a.m. and the fish was a two pound rudd! It took a huge lobworm literally as it touched the surface of the water and my only indication that it was on was a tug on the rod top. It was too dark to see our floats properly unless they were cocked and mine never had the chance to cock at all! I was waiting for it to do so when I felt the pull.

I began to see what Father had meant about getting down past the rudd!

As the light improved we groundbaited the swim heavily and settled down to fish with orthodox tench outfits. Our big lobworms lay hard on the bottom in a swim which had a good bottom carpet of groundbait. Our floats were peacock quills fixed at the bottom end and the single shot was placed about a foot from the hook.

We caught roach, rudd, perch, and small pike for a time and then big sheets of bubbles began to appear in the swim. The tench had arrived and soon we began to catch them. They were big by previous standards. Many were over four pounds – some were over four and a half, and they were clean, sleek and buff coloured, unlike any tench I had seen previously.

It was a great day. We took twelve tench each and went home completely exhausted. We had seen no one during the day at all, for it seemed that those other anglers who had decided to fish on opening day had chosen to fish at the Sawmills. The thought of the long trek to the Warrells had apparently deterred them! Exhausted or not, however, the next morning saw us both at the same swim again at crack of dawn with a new supply of bait and groundbait.

The day that followed was almost a repetition of the previous one. We took another twelve tench each and went home feeling, if anything, even more exhausted!

The tench fishing at the Warrells was easy, we decided, and indeed it was for the greater part of that season. Only towards the end of August did the tench become difficult and it was then that we found it necessary to apply some of our previously gained experience.

Because of the apparent unwillingness of the tench to bite boldly it became necessary to use smaller baits and to fish the lift method. Breadcrust appeared to be the best bait in the circumstances and for some time we enjoyed extremely good fishing when other baits were proving unsuccessful.

We gradually learned the need for a change of bait, however, and it became apparent that in swims which are heavily groundbaited and fished regularly it is an advantage to ring the changes often. We learned the value of big pieces of flake with the edges left ragged, of really well made soft bread paste, of stewed wheat, and of mixed baits such as wheat and maggot or crust and maggot.

We learned also how to fish the lift style properly, something which even our past experiences had not taught us.

I have described the lift method briefly in foregoing chapters and by now the reader will be aware that it is quite different from other more orthodox methods.

I have not described the finer points, however, and as there have been so many new developments on the 'lift' theme allied to a number of new still-water, float-fishing techniques, it may suffice at this stage to point out the main differences between lift and regular float attachments. Later I will describe the method more fully in a chapter devoted to modern float techniques.

The length of peacock quill which serves as the float is attached at the bottom end only with a wide, tight-fitting rubber or latex band. The tackle is set deeper than the water and *all is drawn taut* until the float cocks. That way the depth setting remains constant and the single shot which cocks the float must always remain on the bottom. Lift floats should be over-shotted so that they sink if set too shallow. The rod should remain in rests and the strike is made immediately from the rest with no pause in between. The moment the float lifts or lies flat the rod should be picked up and the strike made in one combined movement. It takes practice, but it is effective. Speed is called for, but there are ways of 'slowing down' certain tench bites, as we shall see later.

In the summerhouse swim we often found ourselves chasing bubbles. That is to say the tench bubbles appeared on the surface here, there and everywhere in the swim at different times. Often, to drop a bait in the middle of a patch of bubbles, meant the catching of a fish, but it was important that we should have the depth setting correct each time because a different line of cast often meant that we were fishing in water a few inches deeper or shallower than

Author fishing at Wotton . . .

previously. The sinking lift float soon gave us the necessary information regarding depth and the rig was quickly adjusted to suit the new conditions.

For the greater part of the time it was sufficient to set the shot about two inches from the hook and to strike immediately the float lay flat, but there were times when it was necessary to use a little more finesse. It was sometimes essential to set the shot only one inch from the hook and to make the strike while the float was actually in the process of lifting in the water. When you consider, as I have already described, that the rod was never held, but always remained in rests, and that the rod had to be picked up and the strike made during that brief split second, it will be seen that our reflexes became highly developed.

One of our favourite baits in these circumstances was puffed wheat breakfast cereal. When bites were few and far between, despite intense activity in the swim, we often found that one grain of puffed wheat would do the trick. To take six or seven tench in a day on this

. . . and into a fish

bait took a great deal of concentration. It was a bait which simply would not stay on the hook for very long. Often the movement of tench or other fish in the swim caused it to come popping to the surface. The strike had to be made the very moment the float began to move and we missed a great many fish because we were too slow. Nevertheless we made contact often enough to make our efforts worthwhile, and although it was extremely hard fishing, I never tired of using puffed wheat. I have no idea why it was so deadly. I can only assure you that it was and that it has accounted for many tench.

We also caught tench on stewed wheat from time to time in the summerhouse swim, particularly when they were bubbling profusely, but it was not until later, when we fished the Sawmills Lake regularly, that we realized why it proved so successful.

Changing from big baits and big hooks to smaller baits on more delicate rigs often meant the scaling down of the tackle in general. For instance, a 6 lb breaking-strain line tied to a no. 6 hook is fine for big lobworms or big pieces of flake or paste in weedy water, but a finer line is needed to fish with a grain of wheat or a tiny cube of crust on a no. 14. Generally speaking we tried to avoid using fine links and preferred to tie our hooks directly to the reel line. This meant that on occasions we were fishing with lines of 2 lb breaking-strain.

I should make it quite clear here that I have never chosen to fish with a weak line for the sake of doing so. There is nothing clever about getting broken and leaving a tench trailing a couple of yards of nylon. The only time I would fish really fine for tench is if I could not catch them any other way. Very often this scaling down of tackle became essential and resulted in catches we would not otherwise have had, but today's 4 lb lines are probably as thin as the 2 lb lines we used then and I seldom find it necessary to go below that strength nowadays. I have pulled big tench through soft weed-beds many times on tackle comprising a no. 16 model perfect hook tied to a 4 lb breaking-strain line. The strength of such tackle and the holding power of such small hooks are quite surprising. Remember, too, that on the occasion when such tackle is used, the object is to defeat the quick bites of tench which will not take a big bait. The strike is very quick and this means that the tench is nearly always lip hooked. The lips of a tench are very tough; so much so that, far from there being danger of the hook coming out, it is often very difficult to remove it after the fish has been landed.

Every tench-fishing situation can have its own particular bait/hook/line-strength problem and there is little I can say about it except to suggest that it is not sensible to tie a no. 4 hook to a 4 lb breaking-strain line, to cover a no. 14 hook with an outsize lobworm or to impale a single grain of wheat on a no. 6.

If I was asked to name an all round useful hook for tench fishing I would choose a no. 10. It is the hook I have used and still use most of all. It will accommodate a worm at a pinch and is useful for crust, paste, flake, wheat or maggots. It can be used with a wide range of line strengths, but it will *not* cope with all tench-fishing situations. It should not be expected to.

Although my brother Ken and I (and later Joe Taylor as well) travelled so as to fish at dawn whenever possible, there were inevitably times when we had to be content with ordinary daytime fishing at the Warrells. It was then that we learned how to catch tench in the margins. We learned that it was not necessarily a waste of time tench fishing during the day when the sun was high. It was true that baited swims seldom yielded fish in those conditions but it was also true that the tench themselves did not necessarily stop feeding.

Very often, when the baited swim was either dead or full of tiny rudd (strange how those appeared when the tench retired, thus letting us know that the situation had changed) there would be a great deal of movement in the marginal reeds; and from the very way the reed stems swayed and shuddered, it became obvious, very quickly, that fish bigger than small rudd were responsible.

I thought it possible that they could be tench and put my baited hook as close to the reeds as I dared. It lay there untouched despite the movement of fish in the vicinity. It seemed, on reflection, that the greater part of the activity was taking place at mid-water or near the surface and by constant watching I was finally able to see the fish.

Occasionally one would swim very close to the surface along the edge of the rush bed and then turn abruptly, directly into it. The rushes swayed. An odd fish showed a fin or a piece of back in the sunlight and eventually I was convinced that tench were present and active.

Could they be feeding? If so, in what manner? I made a guess, and it has never been more than a guess really, that the tench were feeding off the rush stems. I thought, perhaps, that they were taking their food at mid-water and that they were possibly dislodging some of that food with their tails or bodies as they worked their way in and out of the thicket. It seemed to me that they were 'grazing' somewhere above the bottom of the lake.

I tried a number of ways of catching them and finally decided that if food *was* being dislodged from the rush stems it would sink slowly to the bottom. Perhaps the tench were taking it while it was sinking?

Whether my guesses or theories were correct I have no way of knowing except that I *did* catch a lot of tench by fishing slowly sinking baits in, or very close to, those marginal rushes. In those days I used small red worms for a start, but later found that one grain of wheat and one maggot impaled on the same no. 12 or 14 hook was very much more acceptable.

I didn't find this out by accident. It was planned this way.

I thought, perhaps, that the fish food most likely to be found on the rush stems would be small snails and I did in fact find some in later years, but I confess they were very few and far between. The nearest thing to a small snail which I could present was a grain of stewed wheat (not too unlike a snail shell if you use a little imagination) and I added a maggot to give it some life. It worked very well indeed, and became a regular daytime tench-fishing method.

I presented the bait in a number of different ways, but my best result came when the bait was sinking slowly below a small self-cocking float. In these circumstances no long casting was necessary and I was often able to lower the bait from a longish rod. Eventually, I made up a thirteen footer with a butt and middle of tonkin and a full length built cane tip. It would be 'old hat' by today's standards and compared with the latest in modern fibreglass design, but it had one good feature. It was powerful, and it needed to be. Tench had to be extracted from some real trouble spots and there were times when I found it necessary to *push* rather than pull a fish out of trouble. This rod was ideal for the job.

I fished the Warrells for many years and despite the long walk involved often carried a tent, bedding, food and bait for a long weekend.

The best catch I ever had there was eighteen tench, about half of which were over four pounds. Joe Taylor took a five pounder once and there was a report of a six pounder which I could never be quite sure about.

By 1953 it became apparent, after catching hundreds of fish, that we were not likely to catch a really big tench there, and although the three of us still fished it often (Joe Taylor had now joined us on our regular trips and we became known as The Taylor Brothers – although Joe is really a cousin) we felt the need for a new water or a new approach which would get us among the really big fish.

We had not, until then, done anything in the way of pre-baiting swims, nor had we done any night fishing.

Later, at the Warrells we were able to practise night fishing for tench but before that came about we were to gain more experience elsewhere. By this time several boats had been put on the Sawmills Lake and boat anglers had learned that there were even better tench there than at the Warrells.

It came to our notice that an almost derelict hulk of a boat, which had been launched on the lake a year or so previously, had been allowed to deteriorate so badly that the owner wished to sell it. It was an ex-WD pontoon which had been stripped of its internal structure in order to be made into a houseboat, an idea which was eventually abandoned.

Ken, Joe and I split the cost between us and bought it for twenty pounds. It was probably the best bargain we had ever had, and it provided us with a mobile fishing platform which was the scene of many really exciting catches and discoveries in the years to come.

# 6 The Sawmills

By the time we had made our boat serviceable, and had built a folding canopy over the top to allow us to fish in the rain and sleep on board in comfort, the open season was only three weeks away. I do not remember a close season when I worked harder or anticipated the next season so eagerly, for we already had a good idea of what the Sawmills' fishing had to offer. There were two club boats available and on several occasions we had hired one of them to explore the lake and to fish. Our fishing from then on was one round of success. In fact we were probably too successful and at one time became rather blasé about the whole business, but I can say quite honestly that we worked very hard for the wonderful results we achieved.

In those days, the number of tench caught was roughly proportional to the amount of weed clearing done and the amount of groundbait introduced; and we were no sluggards at this sort of thing! We learned as we went along and we tried to associate depth with water temperature, method with tench behaviour and the time of day or time of year. We reached many conclusions; and we formed many theories, most of which worked for us on the Sawmills Lake.

I could write of scores of weekends when colossal bags of tench were taken and I could name many anglers who caught either their first, or their best or their biggest bags of tench when they fished one of our famous pre-baited swims; but these stories would only serve to bore the reader.

We had a happy knack, too, of changing swims at about the right time. Every so often the chosen swim would give up the ghost and stop producing fish. We were always able to anticipate this happening and while others were fishing empty swims we would be engaged in finding, clearing and baiting an entirely new area. And it always worked for us. Throughout the season we changed our swim several times and managed to catch tench right through until the summer was over.

We used many different materials to bait the swims we chose and at times it proved rather expensive, but as we fished every weekend for as many hours as we could, we considered it worthwhile. We felt that, as we were not spending money on anything other than our fishing weekends, we were entitled to be a bit lavish with the bait and groundbait.

Between three of us it was not over-expensive, even though we often bought six dozen loaves at the regular retail price to serve for hookbait and groundbait! During the week, of course, every piece of stale bread we could find was seized and stored, and I was often able to get cartons of stale cake-crumbs and bakery waste from near-by, which helped to eke out the more expensive bread. We would also get a can of oxblood from the local abattoir during the week and allow it to congeal into a horrible jelly-like mass for the weekend. This has been regarded as a super means of attracting tench into a swim for as long as I can remember. It certainly worked at Wotton, but there were times when I am convinced we would have done just as well with ordinary groundbait and no oxblood.

Having, therefore, learned the importance of preparing and pre-baiting swims with the aid of the club boat, we were off to a good start when we had our own. We could then, of course, take it out and work as often as we pleased without making special arrange-ments with the club secretary.

All the while we worked on our boat we watched the water for signs of tench and planned where our first swim would be. Our idea was to anchor the boat and stay there for the first few days of the season. Our holidays had been arranged with this in mind, and because the big pontoon was obviously going to be difficult to handle, especially in a wind, and because continual coming to shore would undoubtedly disturb some of the bank anglers, we organized cooking and toilet facilities on board. They were crude, but nevertheless practicable and just in case a trip to shore was considered essential we acquired an inflatable dinghy which later accompanied us on all our trips to the middle of the lake. It turned out to be a boon, and saved us endless hours of hard work.

The swim we chose for that first weekend was only about three feet deep, and it did not hold a lot of weed. It was a mud-bottomed patch of fairly clear water, surrounded by dense beds of milfoil, Canadian pondweed and curled pondweed. We gave it a preliminary rake over one evening with a light throwing drag and a big pole drag. All we did really was stir up some of the mud on the bottom and introduce some bread and bran groundbait. Within an hour we could see that tench were present. Bubbles began to come to the surface as they worked over the bottom.

That particular swim needed very little more in the way of weed clearance. We 'fed' it with bread and chopped worms two or three times a week and spread the bait over a wider area each time. The cleared hole grew bigger as the tench continued to work over it and soon there were small mats of soft weed floating on the surface where the tench had uprooted it. We had a swimful of tench well before the season opened and in order to encourage more we applied our round-the-clock dragging principle for the first time.

We cleared long narrow channels leading away from the swim like spokes from the hub of a wheel and these channels we kept lightly baited until the evening of 15 June.

We were still not allowed to fish at night, but we considered that it was in order to bait up through the hours of darkness and we took a huge supply of bread, bran and oxblood out with us in the early evening.

Our procedure was simple. Some of the bread was put over the side to soak in a big sack for an hour or so. While this was going on the boat was prepared for the night. Tackle was assembled ready for morning, paste and other baits were prepared, and we each set out our individual 'stalls'.

In those days we tried many different sleeping arrangements but we had finally settled for ordinary deckchairs. These were fine. They took up little room and allowed us to sleep in reasonable comfort across the boat, which was just about 6 feet wide. Sometimes, we would use air beds for a really comfortable night's sleep and when we did so we simply folded the deckchairs flat and made our beds up on top of them.

Mostly, however, we spent a great deal of the night talking, brewing tea, baiting and generally enjoying the summer night. A few hours' doze was all we required and, with our deckchairs set on their lowest notches we were able to rest well enough. At daybreak, by lifting the deckchairs up a couple of notches we were ready to fish in the most comfortable of all angling seats. I am sincere about this. There is no better seat for fishing than a deckchair and I would not consider fishing from anything else if it was practical. Even now I still struggle to get a deckchair to my night-fishing pitch if it is at all possible.

Pat Russell and Joe Taylor weed-clearing from the pontoon

So it was on that first night. Our deckchairs were arranged and the shelf in front of us, which we had built on to the boat, soon held our personal fishing odds and ends as well as three steaming mugs of tea and plates of eggs and bacon. We each cooked our own meals on individual stoves because we had found this to be far the best idea in our limited space.

When the bread had soaked and we were fed, we hauled out the sack and squeezed out the excess water on to the bows by marking time on it! The contents were then transferred to a wooden tub and thoroughly mixed with the blood. The whole mess was then dried off with bran and about a third of it was scattered over the swim. Tench began to 'boil' immediately and throughout the night we fed the area sparingly. More bread meanwhile was left to soak over the sides ready for morning.

At about one o'clock in the morning one of us, I will not say who, decided to break the club rules and put a bait out. It was a big lobworm and it was out precisely one minute before the ratchet on the centrepin reel began to click. Within minutes a four pound tench was in the boat and quickly released. Then feeling very guilty we settled down again to wait for dawn. And what a dawn it proved to be! I shall always remember it. We began fishing at four o'clock and by twenty-five minutes past we had caught twenty-four tench – almost one a minute. If that sounds far fetched let me point out that three anglers were involved and at times we were all playing a tench at the same time. I have never known such action either before or since.

We used lift floats made of the usual few inches of peacock quill cocked by one shot which was placed about a foot from the hook. We used lobworms the whole day through and the bites were decisive runs which took our floats right under. Although we were using lift floats we were certainly not fishing the lift method. On that day it wasn't necessary.

Our total bag for the day was seventy-nine tench – eighty counting the one caught in the night. Only nine of them were under four pounds and several were over five!

We later enjoyed many days when had we tried really hard we could probably have caught the same number of fish again, but that remained our best day ever. There were many days when the bag was only half that amount which gave us just as much, if not more, pleasure.

Our catches received publicity in the angling press and when well known anglers from far and near asked to be allowed to fish with us, we began to think we knew a little about tench fishing.

At that time our fishing was being applied in much the same manner as that suggested by Richard Walker. We had all read *Still Water Angling* and we were Walker fans. It was inevitable that we should meet and fish together before long. Dick finally came with Peter Thomas, stayed a full weekend and caught a fair bag of fish in conditions which were not really conducive to good tench fishing. We have all been the very best of friends ever since.

It had been obvious to both Dick and me, in a correspondence which had been going on for some time, that our approaches to fishing in general were similar. We were giving thought to our tench problems and applying methods to suit them in the same way as

Dick Walker searching for 'natural baits' on his first visit to Wotton

he was dealing with his own particular carp situations. We *did* have problems and they became more and more obvious as each season grew older and each new one came around. We had location problems, we had problems of water temperature, and what Dick and I called preoccupation.

Sometimes the tench would be difficult to locate when we decided to change our swim, but somehow we always managed to encourage *them to find us*. We spent many hours drifting in search of fish and taking the water temperature at certain depths, because we were convinced that temperature played a big part in the tench's whereabouts. Frankly we learned very little except that there is hardly any temperature change of a wide area in a shallow tench lake such as the Sawmills. It was an open lake and the water was well mixed. The bottom temperature in ten feet was seldom different from that in four feet. There were times, in very hot weather, when there was an upper layer of warm water and this was especially noticeable

Peter Thomas hooks an early Sawmills tench . . .

. . . and displays it

where thick weed helped to hold the warmth. Generally speaking, though, we found the thermometer of little use in helping us to locate fish. We did find, however, that in very hot weather many of the tench moved into the deepest water they could find at night, and again when the sun was high. We found too that some tench would move into the upper layer of water, seemingly to enjoy the warmth. Mostly they would lie with their heads hidden under some softweed and it appeared that they liked the shade. Sometimes, when the weather remained very settled and there was no overnight drop in water temperature, some tench would remain active in a small area for days at a time.

We reckoned, at that time, that the ideal temperature for tench fishing was about 64°F, but that a *steady* temperature was better than one which changed greatly from day to day. I still think this is right, but I also believe that the available food supply plays a big part in the tench's whereabouts. Let's face it, no tench is going to stick around for long if no food is available, even if the temperature is perfect! In those halcyon days at Wotton we could always ensure that there was plenty of food!

Perhaps we overdid it. Perhaps, because we and others who were doing the same thing elsewhere in the lake introduced too much unnatural food, the tench became finicky and difficult to catch. Once again we applied lift tactics and once again they worked, so that we could catch plenty of fish.

It was about that time that I discussed this matter with Dick Walker. As I have already shown he had advocated an entirely different technique to deal with the problem of finicky tench bites. His tactics would not work on our waters at Wotton, but I had no reason to doubt his word that they would work on his. Likewise he, too, was puzzled as to why our ideas were so different and why, when applied, they did not deal with the same problem on his particular waters. I know that Dick gave the matter considerable thought. He had fished our waters; we had not fished his and I think he came up with the answer some time later when he wrote:

### *Tench and the lift method*

For the last two years I've been worrying about a curious difference between my tench fishing methods and those employed so successfully by Fred, Ken and Joe Taylor at Wotton Lakes. I'd found that in most of the waters where I fish for tench, it pays to have the lead on the tackle a good distance from the hook. I've watched tench feeding in several of these waters and seen them standing on their heads to pick up a bait.

When they're doing that, they're liable to brush up against a line running from float to shot, or leger-lead, if the bait lies close to the hook. This not only causes a lot of false alarms to be registered by the float, but it can result in the tench actually pulling the bait away from his own mouth, by brushing against the line or washing the line sideways by fin and tail movements. I'm not guessing that this happens; I've seen it, quite often.

The Taylor brothers, however, fish more often than not with one shot, a big swan-shot, about an inch from the hook, and a peacock quill float attached by the bottom end only. They catch plenty of tench, too. They call it the lift method, because the float registers a bite by lifting upwards. It isn't new; it's been used on the Lea for tench, and also big roach, for many years, but it never seemed to claim much interest elsewhere until the Taylors began catching vast numbers of tench with it, as well as other kinds of fish.

I tried the lift method at Wotton, and it certainly works well; but in other places I fish, it isn't very successful, and I'm wondering why. Possibly the nature of the bottom and of the bait may provide some clue.

At Southill Park, one of the places where the lift hasn't seemed to work so well, the bottom is for the most part quite large stones. A bait like a worm or a piece of paste probably rests in a hollow among the stones, and a tench has to stand on his head and try to suck it up. A line rising vertically above the bait would make that difficult.

On the other hand, fishing with crust on a flat bottom, using the lift technique, means that the crust floats up an inch above the shot. A tench need not stand on his head at all to take it. Consequently, he won't be nearly as likely to touch the line. Crust or flake on lift tackle often seems to work better than worm on the same gear; possibly because a worm will try to bury itself in the mud, and a tench would have to dig it out – banging up against the line in the process.

When tench are shy, as they often are by August or even earlier in waters that are heavily fished, you can often catch fish on a level bottom by using the lift method, with smallish baits, and striking at small float movements, when ordinary methods fail. I think it pays when fixing up the tackle, to have a soft shot, pinched on fairly lightly. Then you can put it close to the hook or bread baits, or slide it a foot or so away from the hook if you decide to try worm – or if you get a lot of niggling bites with which you can't connect by striking early, but which never develop into a more definite pull however long you wait.

Any mug can catch tench when they're feeding well and boldly in a straightforward swim; but to catch them consistently means finding where they are at any given time and using the right technique to suit the swim they're in and the behaviour of the fish themselves.

Many an angler says: 'The tench aren't on today' when, had he known enough, he might have had a good bag. It is true there are times when fish won't feed – but they aren't nearly so common as the times when we anglers are too ignorant to catch fish.

And again later:

### *It won't always work*

The first mention of the lift method in print that I ever saw was in a book by the late Ted Ensom ('Faddist') published before the war, where it was described as a favourite method of some Lea anglers who wanted to catch fewer but bigger roach. Ted mentioned that anglers using it caught tench as well, now and then.

At that time I didn't take much notice, of it, as it appeared to offer no advantages over more usual methods of tench fishing, and in many of the waters I fished for tench there were decided objections to having the line rising from the bottom near to the bait.

Those objections I set out in detail in my book *Still Water Angling*. As far as I was concerned, the lift method wasn't a very good idea. It wasn't until I met the Taylor brothers of Aylesbury and went tench fishing with them, that I found that the lift method can be deadly; and it was Fred Taylor who first explained to me exactly when and how to use it.

Like all angling methods, it fails unless it is used in the right conditions and in the right way. When tench are feeding really well, and the bottom is hard and irregular, as it is – for example – at Southill Park, the lift method can be a handicap.

Feeding fish that are practically standing on their heads brush up against your line, and cause movements of bait and float. You either keep striking at false knocks, continually missing and eventually scaring the fish, or else you wait for the solid bite, and seldom get it. Under those conditions, you want at least two feet between hook and shot, and your bait will be quite a large one, like a lobworm, a piece of paste, or paste and crust, or a pinch of flake, pinched hard enough to sink.

Where the 'lift' method really comes into its own is where you have to use small baits, especially over soft bottoms. The time to use small baits is when you can't catch tench on larger ones fished in the orthodox way. I stress that, because you must be sure that the tench have actually refused a big bait, and that the various undecided float movements you may have observed are really due to fish playing with the bait and dropping it, rather than fish brushing against the line, or washing it about.

Having decided that circumstances demand use of the lift style, remember that its main advantage lies in its ability to tell you sooner than do other methods that your bait has been taken, and fish accordingly. You are now trying to catch fish that are likely to take in and spit out your bait, all in a short fraction of time. That is one reason for using a compact or small bait.

True you can use lobworms on lift tackle with some success, but a lobworm is liable to be taken by one end, with the hook outside the mouth of the fish, which causes many missed strikes. The Taylor brothers move their shot to a foot or more away from the hook when they change from flake or crust to lobworm. Flake, crust or maggots, or little red worms, are the bait to use with the lift, baits that a tench can get in his mouth at one suck. As soon as that happens, up bobs your float, and you must not delay striking.

Books and articles dealing with tench fishing generally, advise the angler to delay striking until the float slides under and away, and with conventional tackle this advice is sound. Not so with the lift. This is in essence a method designed to enable you to strike quickly. Since it also demands a rod set in rests, you have to be very 'quick on the draw'.

I think this just about sums it all up and if the reader thinks I have devoted too much space to the lift method I ask him to believe me when I say that it is, to me, the most versatile and useful tench-fishing technique I know. I do not believe it is possible to become an efficient all-round tench fisher without it.

The preoccupation problems arose from time to time when we were faced with a situation guaranteed to drive any angler frantic.

We would sometimes find our swim full of feeding tench. That they were present and feeding was obvious by the large sheets of bubbles which rose to the surface continually. The water would become discoloured, and small pieces of weed or debris from the bottom would often come surfacewards with the bubbles.

In earlier days on other waters, when we saw the bubbles appear, we would chuckle and say 'They've arrived', and we would then proceed to catch them! In later years at the Sawmills this was not the case. Those tench became virtually uncatchable.

We were never sure whether they had decided to feed on the groundbait which their active delving had broken up into tiny particles, or whether, in fact, they were feeding on natural items of food which they were finding in the soft mud. I am inclined to think the latter. I had discussed the problems of preoccupation with Dick Walker several times and I felt that my problem was similar to his. Big fish feeding enthusiastically on many minute identical items of food are apt to ignore or overlook a substantial bait completely. I have many times said it is like a hungry man who is picking blackberries from the hedgerow to sustain him, overlooking a plate of roast beef which someone has placed at his feet! It isn't a very good example, it is possibly a ridiculous one, but I believe it serves to illustrate the point.

Obviously, to catch the fish which are behaving thus it is necessary to wean them off the food they are taking and offer them something else. This is not practical with baits like paste, crust or worms. It could be done with maggots, I'm sure, and I have been successful with maggots in other waters where the same problem exists, but it was difficult at the Sawmills because too many maggots often attracted hordes of small rudd.

I found that stewed wheat was often the answer. I sat, one day,

Wotton today – author returns a tench to the Sawmills lake

dropping grains of wheat over the side of the boat into the clear water. I watched them sink and gradually disappear and it became apparent that they were sinking into the almost liquid mud on the bottom. I had used wheat before with some success and it now occurred to me that the tench would have to take each grain from *out* of the mud rather than off the top of it. Tench, of course, take many other baits in the same way from muddy bottoms, but I saw now that stewed wheat offered a chance of competing with the natural food they were finding. Here was a food made up of many hundreds of identical portions, small, but sinking quite quickly when introduced. Rudd were not particularly fond of it and it settled into the soft oily mud where the tench were 'boiling'.

It didn't always work, but when we were faced with preoccupied tench in future we fished almost exclusively with stewed wheat. We scattered it loosely over a wide area and hoped that eventually the tench would find it and accept it as readily as the natural food they were seeking. Very often they did; and we found that we could then catch several tench, or at least save a complete blank, by using a stewed wheat hookbait. It was necessary, however, to fish with a single grain on a small hook. Several grains on a big hook were invariably left strictly alone. To ensure that the wheat on the hook settled in the surface 'skin' of the mud we put the cocking shot very near the hook and sometimes used one a little heavier than was strictly necessary to cock the float.

Some time after we began to fish the Sawmills we became interested in carp. This came about largely because of the writings of Dick Walker but also because we saw an occasional big carp at Wotton and found four dead ones during the close season. We pressed then for a lifting of the night fishing ban and at the next annual general meeting of the Vale of Aylesbury Association a motion to allow night fishing was passed.

By this time we three were equipped with Mark IV carp rods, fixed spool reels, bite alarms and all the necessary equipment for carp catching, including an enormous landing net made from a cycle wheel rim.

We fished a lot from the boat, largely because all our gear was aboard and it was more convenient to transport it by water to some of the inaccessible spots we chose to fish.

We were always quiet and we worked according to 'the book', but we caught no carp. Our night catches of tench, however, were quite astonishing and, because of this, we took to fishing the baited swims again through the darkness of many nights. Our daytime fishing suffered, but the big tench, fish over five pounds, which we took made up for it.

The baits we used were huge. The tackle was stout, 9 lb breaking-strain line and no. 2 eyed hooks. We never found it necessary to fish finer than that at night and the tench would make long determined runs with paste and flake baits almost as big as hen's eggs!

It always puzzled me why this should happen in the dark when in the daytime it often needed intense concentration to see a sensitive float so much as flicker!

Between the Sawmills and the Warrells was a stretch of water known as the Narrows. In the middle of it was an island known as Grotto Island and we chose this as one of our carp-fishing sites. We caught only tench it's true, but we developed our techniques further, as I will describe later. Meanwhile we were invited to fish for carp and tench at Woldale in Lincolnshire with Maurice Ingham.

# 7 Woldale Lake

I went to Woldale mainly to catch carp, but when I learned that there was a lower lake which held tench I became very interested in it. The carp fishing at Woldale top lake is usually practised at night; very few carp are ever caught during the day, and having finally caught my first-ever double figure carp and followed that up with a few more on subsequent visits, I began to pay more attention to the daytime fishing in the lower lake.

Maurice Ingham, John Ellis and other members of the Tench-fishers Club were at that time very hard at work on several tench-fishing projects, not the least of which was an attempt to catch a big tench from the lower lake at Woldale. They were not having a great deal of success and they paid me a very big compliment when they asked me to see what I could do.

The lower lake is one of the most delightful lakes I have ever fished. It is not large, only four acres or so in extent, but what it lacks in size it makes up for in beauty. It nestles in a deep hollow surrounded by woodland and ferns, and it smells of water mint like all good tench waters should. It is fed by the overflow of the top lake and the water is always crystal clear. It runs from a few inches deep at the overgrown shallow end, to six or seven feet at the deep or dam end. An ancient brick and tiled boathouse holds a leaky boat which is used for weed clearance. Most of the fishable water can be reached from the bank, so there seems to be little point in using a boat for fishing. The most productive swims appear to be those which have been dragged out at the dam end.

I went out at dawn the first time I fished there and found Norman Woodward, a keen tench angler, already fishing with what I considered to be crude tackle and lobworms. In fact I suppose Norman's tackle was no more than adequate for the job in hand. He was fishing in traditional style with tackle slightly heavier than normal because of the particular situation. It was thought that some very big tench lived in the lower lake and Norman wanted to be sure of landing whatever he hooked in the weedy water.

I settled to fish in the next swim, using lift tackle and small crust cubes. I caught a lot of fish but they were all roach, rudd or small bream. Neither Norman nor I caught a tench that morning but later in the day after he had left, I managed to extract a couple of three pounders on small red worms fished close to the thick reed beds. I did not regard this as unusual at the time because I was used to catching tench in this fashion, but I learned later that very few tench were ever caught around midday at Woldale.

Morning and evening sessions brought me a few tench from time to time, but the lift method was by no means as effective there as it was elsewhere. In fact, I found the traditional style of fishing much better and finally reverted to simple float tackle with about a foot of line lying on the bottom. The bites I had were quite decisive and left me in no doubt at all. Some of the tench I caught weighed four pounds but most were slightly below that weight. All in all I learned very little at Woldale and I was not impressed with my catches. I was continually trying to defeat the small roach, rudd and bream, and it seemed that the tench were never present in very large numbers. Had there been more of them I am sure that they would have pushed the smaller fish out of the swim, just as they did at Wotton and elsewhere.

It was not until later that year that we really came to grips with the Woldale tench. Dick Walker, Pat Russell and Maurice Ingham tried an experiment over one long weekend which finally paid dividends. It was something I had always felt the urge to try but which I had not managed to get around to doing at that time.

Collecting a huge supply of fresh-water mussels from around the margins they opened them up and chopped the meat into small pieces. These they added to a goodly supply of mashed bread and meal, which they introduced to one of the cleared swims overnight.

In the morning they baited with whole fresh-water mussels (less shells) and fished with traditional float tackle. They caught some fifteen tench between them and by the time they left that weekend some thirty had been caught and returned.

Peter Thomas searching for mussels at Woldale

I was duly informed of what had happened, and as my next visit was to be one of a whole week's duration, accompanied by my wife and daughter, I made plans accordingly. I would fish only one night for carp; the rest of the time I would fish for tench.

I spent most of my first day at Woldale searching for mussels but by the end of that time I had accumulated enough for several days' fishing both as groundbait and hookbait. I opened the mussels over a bucket of mashed bread so that the juice ran into the groundbait and was not wasted. Mussels have a peculiar but by no means unpleasant smell, and I am convinced that all fish are attracted to it. The stringy pieces of flesh which adhered to the mussel shells were all mixed in with the bread; the firmer pieces, the main body of the mussels, were kept for use either whole or in snippet form as hookbaits.

It was an interesting experience for me. On very rare occasions in the past I had used mussel hookbaits without success and without confidence. The reasons for the lack of success were obvious. Only at such times as the tench were not taking anything else did I ever resort to trying mussels. It is hardly surprising that they were not successful! Had I tried them, perhaps, when the tench were feeding, it might have been a different story, but with tench feeding well there is never any need to resort to untried and unproven baits.

From this I thought it fair to conclude that only when fish had become accustomed to finding mussels liberally spread over the swim, would they accept them as normal and feed on them. To some extent this is true, but in later years I learned that massive pre-baiting programmes were seldom necessary even in waters where mussels had not been used as bait or groundbait. Indeed, after my experiences at Woldale I found I could often catch tench at the Warrells and Sawmills when the water temperature was well into the seventies Fahrenheit and the tench seemingly not feeding at all. Mussels became a very useful bait when the fish were proving dour, possibly fed to the gills, and cautious of bread, worms and other angler's baits. They took fish when other baits failed both by day and by night and I was very glad (and very secretive) about the plentiful supply of mussels I found at Wotton later.

Opening the mussel shells proved difficult at first until I learned the secret of running a sharp knife between the shells so as to cut the muscle at either side of the 'hinge'. With this muscle severed, the shell opened cleanly and the contents could easily be removed.

Opening a mussel by cutting the two 'hinge' muscles

The supreme tench bait at Woldale – a whole mussel

It was not a fast and furious type of fishing, but the bites came regularly enough to keep me interested. To begin with I used float tackle but, as the mussel baits were subjected to all sorts of pecks, tweaks and pulls from small fish, all of which made the float behave in the most exasperating fashion, I eventually began fishing with a lightly shotted floatless tackle. The bait was still subjected to the attentions of small unwanted fish, but the twitching of the line was not as distracting as the gyrations of the float had been previously. When a bite came, the line usually tightened and stripped off the fixed spool reel, giving plenty of indication. The fish were well hooked and I do not remember losing one because of a poor hook hold. Occasionally, however, a tench would pick up the bait and swim towards the bank with it, giving no noticeable registration on the line. This usually happened towards dusk when the line was difficult to see in the poor light. To overcome this I had to use an unnecessarily large leger lead; one which remained still on the bottom while allowing free passage of line. I chose a three-quarter ounce Arlesy bomb and set it about two feet from the hook. From then on every bite, irrespective of which direction the fish took, was registered by the line peeling off the spool of the reel.

Sometimes, for an hour or so after dark I used either silver paper indicators or electric bite alarms to detect bites.

My daughter Valerie, who was at that time only eleven years old and who should, perhaps, have been a boy, spent most of her time bird-nesting, exploring, rowing the leaky boat and climbing trees, but on occasions she deigned to fish with me. She did not like to sit for long hours waiting for a bite from a big fish and because of this I usually allowed her to use my three piece Avon type cane rod baited with a small mussel snippet. On it she would catch rudd and small bream until she tired of it and went on another 'exploration'.

One morning, however, she saw me catch a number of big tench and decided that she, too, could be patient for long enough to catch one herself. I gave her the Avon rod, baited with a big mussel, and told her where to cast. By this time she had learned to catch small fish very nicely and to handle tackle reasonably well, but because I wanted her to land a big fish if she hooked one, I had put on a heavy line in place of the usual one of about 4 lb breaking-strain. In fact I had grossly overlined the rod. Perhaps it was as well I did for some time later the line stripped off the spool and Valerie struck into her first ever tench. I'm afraid she hauled it in a bit unceremoniously!

Valerie with her Woldale tench

It came thrashing across the top of the water into my waiting net – a fish of well over four pounds if I remember correctly. It was then that I was really glad I had had the foresight to change the line. Had I not done so the fish would have escaped and a very young angler would have been very disappointed!

My main fishing times at Woldale were early mornings, between five o'clock and nine o'clock, before I was called into the cottage for breakfast. These were my serious fishing attempts. During them I tried to catch tench and only tench, and my score by the end of the week was over forty fish ranging from three to four and a half pounds. After supper in the evenings, however, I used to fish for fun and anything that happened along.

I had a very light soft-actioned fly rod with me and I used this as a bait rod most evenings to catch roach, rudd and small bream. My line was only 3 lb breaking-strain, my float a tiny piece of quill. My hooks were no. 14 and my baits were mussel snippets. What fun it was to catch fish on such tackle! Even small fish gave me good sport and on the one or two occasions when I hooked into moderate tench, I suffered many anxious moments.

I have never been sure about the existence or otherwise of unusually big tench in Woldale. I think perhaps there were one or two really big ones present at that time and there had been reports in the *Anglers News* of a nine pounder a few years previously. Maurice Ingham reported seeing some big tench there one year and I once spotted a huge fish which may have been a tench, but I could not be really certain. I always *hoped* that one would come along but I never felt confident that there were fish present much bigger than those I had caught. At least not until the last evening of my stay.

My luggage was packed ready to leave in the morning, but my fly rod and reel were still assembled. I went down to the dam after supper as usual and began to catch fish. They were nearly all bream around the pound mark but there was a sprinkling of very fair rudd also. A bite not different from the rest took me unawares while I was rolling a cigarette, and my hasty strike connected with a really big fish. It tore out to the edge of the swim and bored deeply. I had to give line and more line and still more line. Eventually, because I had no control over it whatsoever, it became weeded and solid. I pulled as hard as I thought the fine line would allow me to, and presently the hook came back to me. I'm glad the tackle didn't break, for I do not like leaving hooks in fish. But I was sorry to lose that one.

What *kind* of fish it was I shall never know. It might have been a lone carp from the top lake, it might have been a pike or a big eel, but it didn't *feel* like any of those. I like to think that it was the record tench that Maurice and John were after and that it is still there to be caught!

Since those early days I have caught carp, tench, and other fish from many waters on mussels and mussel portions without any preliminary baiting. I have never found any cause to believe that tench will take large, whole mussels, including shells, but of course, they *have* been found in large carp. It is reasonable to assume that a big tench will take – say – a walnut-sized mussel and it is an undisputed fact that they will take large water snails and smaller 'pea mussels'.

How they dispose of the hard shells remained something of a mystery until a reader wrote to me at *Angler's Mail* suggesting that the meat was absorbed by the fish's digestive juices and that the shells were then regurgitated. This reader had made a study of many aquarium-housed fish and I feel sure that his suggestion was correct.

# 8 The Narrows

It was still largely with thoughts of carp on our minds that we decided to fish the Narrows, and in particular Grotto Island. The water there was very shallow, very weedy and very unpopular with other members of the Vale of Aylesbury Angling Association, and because we were convinced that carp preferred that end of a lake least frequented by humans, we decided to night fish in the Narrows for most of the late summer.

Grotto Island, so called because it held an artificial grotto built of stones, lath and plaster, was decorated with many thousands of shells, and pieces of coral, and was strategically situated at the shallow end of the Sawmills lake. Its position, in the middle of the shallows, formed the start of what had always been known as 'the Narrows', for it divided the lake into two narrow strips of water which met and finally tapered into one narrow channel running westwards to overflow into the Warrells.

The banks on both sides of the Narrows were swampy and overgrown with reeds, but Grotto Island was firm. It was heavily treed but it was no great task for us to cut pitches and a mooring for the boat. From it we could fish any number of swims, all of which were impossible to reach from the banks proper.

All our gear, food, stoves, tackle, bait, etc. was kept on board the boat and it was a simple matter to transport it all to the island and unload it on the side opposite to that from which we were going to fish. In fact we only unloaded tackle, bait and deckchairs. The rest we left on board, under its permanent canopy, so that we could retire for tea, soup, or a meal whenever we felt the need (which was usually quite often).

The pitches we cut were large ones, so that we could all three (Ken, Joe, and I), sit close together and converse during the night. We were quite ruthless in the cutting down of bushes and bankside

Pushing out to Grotto Island

vegetation, for we felt that no cover would be needed during the night. The ground was covered with moss and ground ivy, and there were philadelphus, laurel, and lilac shrubs around us as well as the large elms and oaks which had been planted many years ago. It was a very pleasant spot, well suited to night fishing, and we hoped to make history on the very first night we fished there.

No one, so far as we could ascertain, had ever caught a carp from Wotton Lakes. They had been seen at odd times and the old estate keepers, now retired, talked of 'shoals of carp like little pigs playing in the narrows'. Our appetites were whetted. We had the tackle, the bait and the time. We thought we had the know-how too.

*Figure 2* Balanced paste and crust bait

Because the Narrows were weedy and muddy we used what was at that time a popular bait for carp – balanced paste and crust. Sufficient paste was built up round a crust-baited no. 2 carp hook to cause it to sink slowly and rest lightly on the soft mud or weedy bottom. Our rods were Mark IV carp rods. Our reels were fixed spools loaded with 9 lb breaking-strain line. Our fine wire, round bend, straight eyed, especially sharpened carp hooks were tied direct. We used no leads or floats because none was necessary.

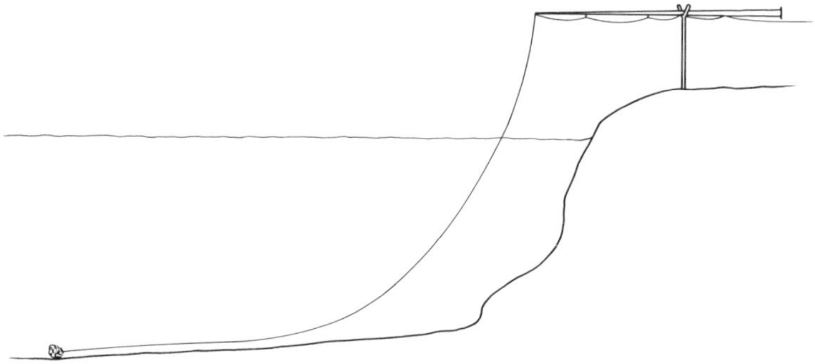

*Figure 3* Simple floatless and leadless tackle

Because of our intense eagerness to catch carp, we had each made two identical electric bite alarms. By today's standards, and by those designed by Dick Walker at that time, they were bulky and crude. They were long wooden boxes which housed buzzer, battery, antenna and light, and they were completely self-contained. We made them thus because we intended to use them from the boat and we particularly wanted to avoid lengths of flex trailing from the rod rest to the buzzer unit. We found them very reliable, and, as they did not have to be transported great distances, the fact that they were bulky did not matter. Certainly, in my opinion, they were easier to maintain and less likely to go wrong than smaller and more sophisticated units. When used on the bank they could be clipped on to straight bank-sticks and although all six held identically sounding buzzer units, a small red light glowed as soon as contact was made, and indicated immediately which alarm was sounding.

On that first night we fished only one rod each because we had insufficient room to fish with two. Later we enlarged the pitch on the western side (which had by then become our favourite) to accommodate two rods apiece.

We cast our baits only a few yards out from the bank and settled back to await results. We had not groundbaited heavily for fear of attracting tench, but we had broken open a new loaf and pinched the inner crumb up into walnut-sized pieces and had scattered them around in our respective hookbait areas.

We had finished our preparations long before darkness fell, but after we had had a cup of tea in the boat it was dark enough to start.

Baits were recast, bite alarms set and the bale arms of our fixed spool reels were opened to allow free passage of the line in case a carp should take. We put on our warm clothing and settled back in our deckchairs to await results. We were deadly serious in our desire to catch carp and we tried very hard not to do things wrong. We shielded our cigarettes, we moved silently and our voices were reduced to whispers, but despite our efforts the whole venture was an anticlimax. Oh we caught fish all right! Dozens of them, but they were tench, not carp!

In the first hour of darkness Ken's buzzer sounded and line began slowly to strip off his reel spool. We had never seen a bite like it before and I remember babbling something about this most definitely being a carp run and to take it easy and not to get excited and so on until Ken picked up the rod and struck. It is to his credit that he remembered to do things right; to snap home the bale arm before striking and keep cool in the midst of my excited ravings. The moment he hooked the fish, however, he informed us that this was yet another tench. A tench that had taken a huge piece of balanced bait and stripped ten yards of line off the spool. A very different kind of bite from those lift bites we were used to experiencing by day in the lake proper! It weighed five pounds.

So it went on all night. Each bite produced another tench and all of them were of remarkably good quality. Many were over five pounds, and it didn't take us long to realize that we were not going to catch any carp that night! In fact, we never did catch carp from the island although we fished for them many times.

It was disappointing, of course, but although we lost out as far as carp are concerned, we gained some invaluable tench-fishing experience, and we became human again. It was never our nature to be as deadly serious as we had become. We had reached a stage when we were not enjoying our fishing and I for one am glad that we regained our sanity and began to put to good use what we had learned. Night fishing for tench then became a most pleasant pastime and later in the season, when the regular tench swims were yielding practically nothing, we would often release a netful of tench first thing in the morning.

It seems rather strange to me that tench should frequent shallow weedy water during the night. One would expect the shallow water to cool quickly and the weed present to give off sufficient carbon dioxide after dark to make things so unpleasant for the tench that they would move out to the deeper weed-free water. In fact this seldom happened. There were times when we could see tench actively working in the shallows by day, as we shall see later, but my impression most nights was that more tench moved into the shallows after dark than moved out of them. Only on really clear, cold nights, and particularly when the moon was full, was there any shortage of tench. In those conditions bites ceased soon after midnight and there were no more then until daylight.

After using balanced paste and crust baits almost exclusively for several nights we tried using the big flake and paste baits I mentioned in Chapter 6. We noticed no difference in the bites we had nor in the number of fish we caught, and when we tried big lobworms and fresh-water mussels we caught good tench on those too.

Night fishing for tench was fun in those days and still is today. I practise it whenever I have the opportunity or when I feel that my chances are better than they would be by day, a situation which is perhaps not easily recognized.

I would hesitate to say what should influence one's decision to fish at night, because waters vary so much in character that the behaviour of the fish varies tremendously. I am sure of one thing, however. Some of the greatest tench fishing of all is to be had at night in waters where the fish are harassed during the day by boating enthusiasts, water skiers, swimmers and the like. Many anglers keep away from such waters because they cannot associate the quiet contemplation of tench fishing with the noisy disturbance caused by other water sports and the arrogance of some of those who practise them. My advice to them is simple. Stay away from such waters by day. Do not even bother to waste time fishing for an hour or so at dawn, for you will find, in many cases, that the fish will not feed in daylight. Fish instead at night, and enjoy the quiet solitude of the waterside after dark. Do not go alone unless you are a confirmed night owl, but go rather with a good companion with whom you can share this rather special pleasure.

Night fishing for tench, you see, is not a deadly serious affair. It will not be necessary for you to talk in whispers, nor will it matter too much if you shine a light or drop your tackle box. Tench will get over these minor disturbances quite quickly whereas the carp could remain alarmed all night.

Although many of the early tench I caught at night were taken with the help of an electric bite alarm, I no longer consider such aids necessary. One hopes for a number of bites during the night from tench and there is usually enough activity to keep one alert. Bite alarms, which shatter the peace of the night, are acceptable to me only as aids to carp fishing, which is generally slower and more demanding than tench fishing.

There are many suitable rigs for tench fishing at night but it is always advisable to keep tackle as simple as possible. Probably the floatless, leadless tackle already described is as good as any, but there is a case, very often, for incorporating a single shot and a float cap. The reason for them is simple. Bites by day may be delicate and finicky, but by night they may be bold and confident. The angler who fishes for tench at night and also likes to fish in the evening and early morning has to use both float and floatless tackles. The simplest answer is to set up a lift tackle in the evening and fish with it until the float can no longer be seen. Then it is a simple matter to remove the float and carry on fishing with the float cap and single shot still on the line. When daylight comes again the float can be replaced without taking down the tackle.

Float tackle *can* be used at night, however, and I will discuss the business of fishing with an illuminated float later in connection with another water where this method is remarkably successful. For the time being, for the purpose of bite registration, I do not believe it is necessary to use anything other than a 'dolly' of some kind or other placed on the line between the reel and butt ring. That 'dolly' can be a piece of paste, a piece of silver paper or one of the very latest, sophisticated, luminous bobbins.

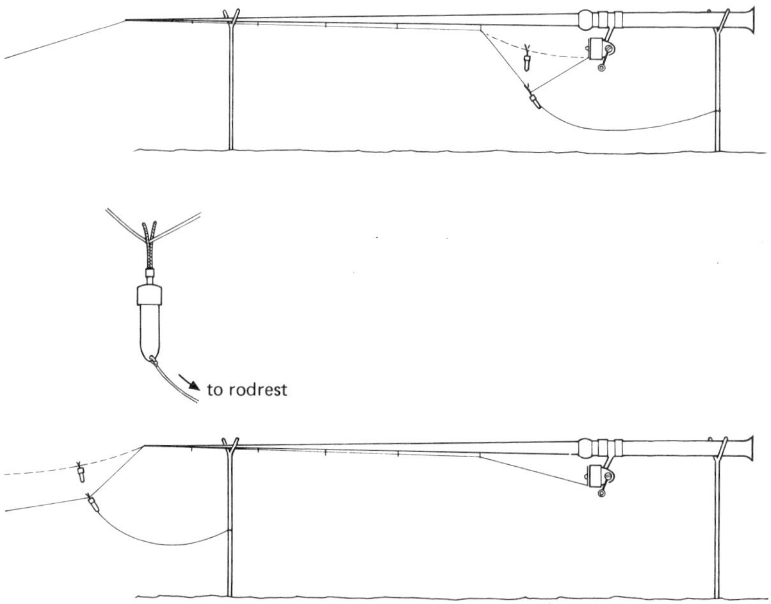


*Figure 4* Two methods of attaching the luminous glow-bob

If one of these expensive 'glow-bobs' is used, however, it is essential to anchor it to a rod rest or ground peg by means of a piece of strong line. The suddenness of any strike will cause the 'glow-bob' to fly off the line and while it may be easily located in the darkness on the bank, the chances are that it will be last seen sailing into the lake to be lost for ever.

I have found that a piece of thin white level fly line is ideal for anchoring the 'glow-bob'. It does not tangle easily and can be seen easily in the darkness.

The source of power contained in a 'glow-bob' is usually referred to by the trade name of beta light. Those in the 'glow-bob' are low-powered but in recent years, high-powered beta lights have become available. They are expensive but they are visible at long range. So much so that we can now, at last, set up a reliable luminous float rig. The developments in this field have been exciting and rewarding. Again, Dick Walker pioneered the whole idea, and despite doubts from many people (myself included) who had struggled to produce luminous floats from low-powered beta lights, once again he proved his point. My experiences with high-powered beta lights are described later in this book.

Tench in some waters tend to move into the bank at night and it is a good idea to use two rods and cover the water close in as well as that farther out. Where eels are present it is as well not to use lobworms unless you are prepared to keep tying in fresh hooks all night. The same can be said about oxblood. Groundbait the area you are going to fish by all means, but if eels are present leave out the blood!

There were very few eels at Wotton and we never encountered any in the Narrows, but we picked up the odd one here and there in blood-baited swims when we fished at night elsewhere. I mention this in case it should be thought that we only fished the shallow weedy water at night. Many times we fished regular swims, both from the boat and the bank, with varying degrees of success, but it was in the Narrows that we really learned how to fish at night and how to enjoy our fishing.

I cannot close this chapter without describing one or two of the funnier incidents which took place from time to time on Grotto Island.

The first one was when Joe, who was using a silver paper indicator pressed lightly into the ground about four feet from his rod, had what he thought was a bite. The silver paper rustled in the darkness, moved a few inches towards his rod and stopped. Joe, after a few moments, decided to tighten the line again, by putting the silver paper back in its original position. He leaned down to do so and picked up a grass snake by the middle! I do not know who was the most scared, the snake, Joe, or Ken, in whose lap it landed when he threw it! We had a lot of trouble with Joe after that. He always wanted to switch lights on to see if snakes were present!

On another occasion a squirrel (how did *that* get on to the island?) jumped from a tree in the darkness and landed on Ken's shoulder. His heart didn't *really* stop; he only said it did! We nearly had trouble with him too that night, but he recovered. And later we both chuckled when Joe, thinking Ken and I were asleep, saw the squirrel again and spent half an hour talking to it and feeding it half a loaf of bread!

As I have already said, Grotto Island was a complete failure as a carp pitch, but it taught us a lot about tench at night. It cured us of our carp fever and by the end of that season we were normal again. As normal as we shall ever be, that is.

# 9 The Island

Having learned something about night fishing for tench and feeling the urge to 'spread our wings' a little, Ken, Joe and I accepted an invitation to join Dick Walker and Maurice Ingham for a few days' fishing in Bedfordshire. The water we fished was noted for its tench and had produced a number of fish over six pounds and at least one seven pounder. It was made up of a series of large pits, most of which were connected by channels. The water was clear, and in many places it was twenty feet deep. It held an abundance of both soft and broad-leaved weeds, and there were extensive shallows. The banks were badly overgrown in places and progress along them was difficult. It was a popular water and one where it was almost impossible to enjoy seclusion.

Unlike Wotton Lakes, where baited swims were 'honoured' and left strictly for those who had baited them, here it was a case of 'first come first served' and it was obvious from the outset that we would have to stay with our swim once we had baited it. Dick and Maurice came up with the solution before we arrived and, with the aid of a small rubber dinghy, commandeered a small island away from the more popular banks and settled in with the equipment necessary for a two-day stay. It was only a tiny island and there was hardly room for us all to fish but we managed to share swims as only really close friends can.

Those two days were not a great success as far as numbers of tench were concerned but I'm sure we all learned a little more about tench. Dick, for instance, caught a good fish, five pounds ten ounces to be exact, in less than a foot of water during the night. That fish came right in to the bank and almost turned over on its side to get at the bait. My night-fishing tactics failed. So did those of Ken and Joe. Our groundbaiting did not attract the fish we expected and it soon became obvious that here the situation was different from what we had been experiencing in recent years.

We were more or less back to square one again. By this I mean that we found the tactics we had used so many years ago in the pits were the ones which paid off here. Bread seemed to be the best hookbait. Groundbait did not really help matters. On reflection, I suppose they were similar situations. The two waters were alike in depth, bottom, weed growth and fish population. The only differences lay in the size of water and the size of the tench.

I further found out that the lift method, in which I had had so much confidence for all those years, was not very suitable here. The float would lie flat when a tench took the bait, but to strike then almost invariably meant a missed fish. I learned to restrain myself when the white quill rose up in the water and keeled over, and to wait until it moved slowly and purposefully away afterwards. That way I caught some fish, the best of which was five and a half pounds.

Some time later, Dick, Joe and I moved over to the island and pitched a tent for several days. It was in the middle of a heat wave. The sun shone mercilessly for the whole of our stay, the water temperature was in the upper seventies and we slowly roasted on the bank.

We caught no fish by day and very few by night, but we were able to *see* some remarkable fish.

The amazing thing about those few days was the way the tench (and I can only assume that they *were* tench) would eat the groundbait overnight and leave our baited hooks strictly alone. One morning very early, Dick and I watched a big tench (I would estimate at least seven pounds) eating the groundbait in great mouthfuls. But it left the hookbaits untouched!

Another time, in the evening, as the sun sank and gave us some welcome shade, Joe and I watched a huge tench roll and jump clear of the water in the vicinity of our motionless floats. We turned to look at each other and we both realized that we had seen the same thing. We spoke in whispers, such was the effect that awesome sight had had upon us. I am not concerned with what others say or think, I *know* that fish must have weighed twelve pounds. And so does Joe!

I tried very hard during those few days to find some answer to the problems we faced on the island. I swam around and took the water temperature in many places hoping to find a spot where the tench might accumulate, but although I found a very wide range of temperatures in the deeps and shallows, I found no real 'hot spot'.

I never fished the island again. The moment we left it, it was occupied by another group who were obviously of the opinion that we had found a magic spot and were determined to make sure that they beat us to it every weekend from then on. Little we cared!

We had enjoyed our stay there but there seemed to be little advantage in the seclusion the island offered and, truth to tell, the regular bank space offered better opportunities for short-term fishing. By using tackle a little finer than usual, and baiting lightly rather than heavily, we took a moderate number of tench with a lot less trouble.

We caught no really big fish but we left the island knowing a little more about how tench sometimes behave at night. That one tench which Dick caught in the very shallow margin added another interesting item of information to our increasing store of tench fishing knowledge. I was able to put that little piece of information to good use in later years as we shall see.

# 10 Arlesey Lake

Arlesey Lake was not far away from the island and a couple of weeks later Dick, Bob Rutland and I fished there.

Bob had been working on the water for a long time knowing that there were good tench present but finding them hard to locate because of the nature and extreme depth of the lake.

The year previously Dick had tried out our 'Wotton tactics' there and had pre-baited a swim heavily with bread and meal, chopped worms and oxblood before the season opened. By opening day the swim was full of fish, but they were perch, not tench. I do not know the exact number of perch he and Bob caught by fishing the swim alternately over several days, but I know it was considerable. I know, too, that this is the only time on record that the perch of Arlesey were caught in any numbers during the summer months.

What had happened, seemingly, was that the bait had attracted the small fish and these, in turn, had attracted the perch. Strange how no tench turned up at all.

Now Bob had changed tactics. He had chosen a swim on the opposite side of the lake where there was a good margin of rush and where the water a couple of rod lengths out was around twelve feet deep. He had baited it regularly after dark and for reasons of secrecy was fishing it at night. Dick and I joined him and Pete Thomas there after dark one Friday night.

Bob explained that the bait he had had most success with was a big lobworm, and we all four dug into his generous bucket and helped ourselves!

At that time I was using a Mark IV Avon rod which allowed me to cast a big lobworm with no shot at all, and I let the bait sink slowly under its own weight about fifteen yards out. For a time I sat and watched a silver paper indicator but, as I had been working hard since the early hours of the morning and had had a particularly busy day, I knew that I would eventually have to snatch a couple of hours sleep. The silver paper danced in the light breeze. I pulled off a little more line, pressed the foil lightly into the mud and stared at it intently. Soon it became two and I blinked them back into one again, but my eyes were heavy and they began to close. The foil rustled along the ground. I grabbed the rod and struck and fairly soon Dick put the big net under a three and a half pounder. Things livened up then and it was not long before all three other rods had caught fish. I lost the urge for sleep temporarily and although I had had no more fish myself I was pleased when the total score reached nine.

Then tiredness overcame me and I dropped off to sleep. I clipped the line into an electric bite alarm before doing so, however, in the hope that I could waken in time to strike if a fish should take.

A moorhen 'bleeped' near my ear. I jumped up but relaxed immediately, realizing that I had been fooled, as I had been fooled so many times before, by the high pitched call of that quaint but rather likeable and friendly water bird. Then the alarm shrilled in earnest and I sat up blindly groping for the rod. It wasn't there. Dick thrust the handle into my hand and said, 'Here, Fred – it's yours.'

I stood up, fell over, and stood up again trying hard all the time to shake myself into wakefulness. The fish pulled away to my right and I instinctively applied sidestrain to keep it out of the rushes. When it finally came towards the net I woke up properly! Dick netted it for me and we weighed it there and then because it was above average size. It weighed five pounds two ounces and turned out to be the season's best for Arlesey Lake. But whose fish was it? Mine or Dick's?

Would I have hooked it had Dick left the rod for me to pick up? Would Dick have landed it on my tackle? And anyway – does it really matter? What really mattered was that ten good tench were caught that night from a water where they did not normally turn up in such numbers. It was perhaps more a triumph for Bob than for us, because it was he who had put in the work and the thinking which made the catch possible. Undoubtedly the floatless leadless rig was the best we could have used on that occasion and it was noticeable once again that the bites after dark were bold runaway affairs which fairly stripped line from the reel spools.

As daylight approached, however, we all four decided without any discussion whatever to use float tackle for the remainder of the session. We caught two more tench, making twelve in all, but we missed several more and it was soon apparent to me that the bites were now fast, delicate, even finicky things which needed a deal of concentration to hit. Why the feeding behaviour of tench should change so drastically in so short a time is something I shall never really understand. It doesn't happen on all waters, nor does it happen on all tench-fishing occasions, but it is as well to remember that such things *do* happen – very often indeed.

I am of the opinion that it is largely a waste of time leaving a big bait out on a floatless or leger tackle after first light. I do *not* suggest that it is not a good method for catching *some* tench in *some* situations, but I firmly believe that to do so means a long wait which could be put to much better use catching tench by more delicate means.

# 11 The Clay Pits

I joined the club that holds the fishing rights on the clay pits just outside my home town after a long time on the waiting list. I was only interested in the carp there because I had heard stories of big fish which could not be caught and I particularly wanted to have some carp fishing near to home where I could watch and study carp behaviour. For a whole season I never bothered to fish there but I *did* spend a lot of time watching; time which finally convinced me that if I ever caught a seven pounder there I would be lucky.

The pits were not big by any means. It was easy to cast across any one of them from any given point, and I soon learned roughly where the carp spent most of their time, where they travelled during the day and where my best chance of catching them would be.

To make a long story short I set to work on them the next season and caught thirteen in six fishing sessions. Only twice did I fish for them very early in the morning and on both of these occasions I caught three. My best was a six and a quarter pounder and I caught that one several times!

It was only through my carp fishing that I learned about the tench in the clay pits, and when I became convinced that I had caught their biggest carp at that time, I turned my attention to the smaller but nevertheless very interesting tench. I began to take tench regularly from the shallow margins and later from off the surface of the water.

Sitting very quietly, hidden by the tall rushes, I fished for carp and watched the tench browsing in among the reed stems right at my feet. I had learned to catch tench in the margins on small baits at Wotton, and I knew that I could expect them here too, but whereas at Wotton my only indication of their presence was the movement of the reeds and rushes as the tench passed between the stems, here I could see them and watch them feed.

I remembered the tench Dick Walker had caught on the island and

I broke up some wet bread pieces to feed the water at my feet. The bread sank, but remained clearly visible, and it was not long before a tench wallowed its way across the shallows to take a piece of bread which was only a few feet from the bank.

I knew then that I could catch one quite easily by putting a hook into the next piece of bread I threw in. I had no real heart for it, however, because the tench were not big and on carp tackle they stood no chance, but, of course, I had to try it! I caught my tench, a two pounder, and promptly put paid to any further hopes of a carp that day, but I thought perhaps I might develop this kind of tench fishing further and have more fun with finer tackle where the situation allowed it.

It was not easy to find a spot away from the dense margins where I might see the tench and fish for them without myself being seen, but I finally managed it from an old wooden staging which had been put up in the shallow water on the far side of the biggest pit. Here the water was no more than two feet deep and apparently actively worked by tench. By using very white bread I was able to see the bait all the time and by wearing polaroid spectacles I was able to see the fish when they arrived.

Problems were always present, of course, in the shape of hundreds of small rudd, which tore all but the toughest baits to shreds a few moments after they had been introduced, but by squeezing up my new bread flake very tightly, I usually found it would last out until a tench found it. The many small rudd attacking it blotted it out from time to time, of course, but sooner or later the shadow of a tench would cause them to 'break ranks' briefly. But they never went away completely as they did whenever a carp appeared, and there were, in fact, a few occasions when their sudden disappearance warned me of an approaching carp which I was sometimes able to catch as a bonus.

I liked this form of fishing. I always think it's exciting to catch a fish you can see, and to watch any fish take the bait is, to me, infinitely better than waiting for the line to twitch and run out. It was here, and later at a smaller and much less significant water, that I first began to catch tench on floating crust. Nowadays I do it regularly because this is one situation where I really can see the fish take the bait.

I am quite sure, of course, that there are many waters where you could fish for a lifetime with surface baits without ever catching a

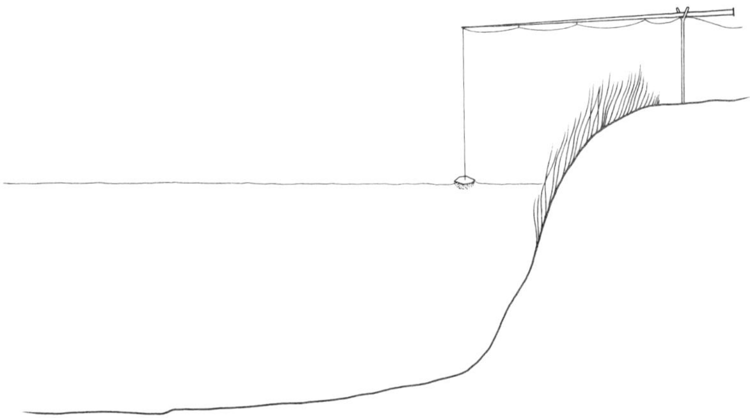

*Figure 5* Surface crust fishing below the rod tip

tench, and if you can catch them on the bottom I suppose there's not much point in wasting good fishing time trying to make things difficult. But it *is* good fun.

Every carp angler knows the nervous tension involved when a big mirror or common swims round and round a piece of floating crust, or lies glaring at it with its mouth adrool, not knowing whether to risk it or not. We've all known the exasperation of seeing a big carp knock a floating bait off the hook and nonchalantly eat the small pieces as they begin to sink. Surface tench fishing isn't quite as exciting as that, but the fact remains that there are waters and situations where surface and near-surface crust baits offer what is probably the best chance of catching tench.

I do not really know why the tench in some waters decide to feed on the surface, but there are one or two factors common to the clay pits and the other water I have mentioned and they might help explain this unusual behaviour to some extent. On the other hand, is it really strange behaviour? Would all tench feed more often on the surface if they were encouraged to do so? I doubt it, but there must be many waters where the possibility has not even been considered and if the situation is such that the tench have been written off as 'nigh impossible', then I feel there is a case for trying the surface bait.

The common factors in the clay pits and the other small water are:

1 the presence of rudd which feed on the surface the moment a piece of bread is thrown in;
2 the complete absence of big predators;

3 both waters have an absolutely foul smelling bottom all over; and
4 they are both shallow (not more than eight feet deep) and less than an acre in area.

The only *un*common factor that I can see is that only one of them holds carp. I can appreciate only too well that fish can 'teach' each other. The carp over the years probably 'learned' from the rudd that surface crust was good food and later, when more and more crust was left floating for the carp, the tench probably jumped on the band wagon too. That's how I've always figured it anyway, and with no prowling pike to contend with, I can well believe that the tench (a lot smaller than the carp and obviously in more danger from predators) would be just as happy as the other species to get their food from anywhere and everywhere.

But I think there is more to it than that. In certain parts of both waters the fish behave rather differently, in that they seldom, if ever, feed on the bottom. I firmly believe that the very foulness of the decaying matter and the black oozy slime really deters them from digging into it for food. Even the seemingly half-starved rudd seem to jib at bottom-fished baits and that helped stimulate my interest in surface baits for tench. I knew, from past experience, that it was possible to catch tench in the margins on slowly sinking baits, and that it wasn't *always* advisable to have the bait lying on the bottom.

I knew, too, as I have already explained in previous chapters, that there were occasions when a cube of crust, anchored down with a big shot, but nevertheless floating a few inches above it because of its buoyancy, was a much better bait than a piece of paste or a worm lying hard on the bottom. And by juggling around with the length of the link between the bait and the shot I found it was possible to catch tench at all depths from time to time. For a long time I went to a lot of trouble making up balanced paste and crust baits that sank very, very slowly and it was not unusual to take several tench from the clay pits when the bait was about six inches below the surface. But I confess that I was fishing for carp when I caught my first tench right on the surface.

Since then I have taken them on baits suspended from the rod tip and barely touching the water at all. I have taken them on baits actually lapping against the bank and in water so shallow that they have had to turn over on their sides to reach them. None of my tench taken this way has been very large, but they've all been a lot of fun to catch.

Had I not fished the clay pits it is doubtful if I would ever have had the experience of catching tench on the surface. Nor would I have thought of using potatoes for bottom baits. Which is something else again and, perhaps, worth recording here.

When I was first fishing the clay pits for carp in conditions which indicated a bottom bait, I experimented for some time with small potatoes, parboiled in the traditional carp-fishing style. I pre-baited and caught many common carp on potato hookbaits, but I also had many runs both in daylight and darkness which did not result in anything other than lost baits. They were not bold runs, but rather jerky stop-and-start affairs which held me puzzled at first.

Then the penny dropped! Just as the tench had learned to take floating crust intended for the carp, so had they learned that potatoes were good food too. The trouble was that they were having difficulty in taking the large portions and golfball-sized whole potatoes that I was using for hookbaits.

It had always been my practice to break a number of potatoes up into small pieces and include them with the bait-sized portions every time I pre-baited. Obviously the tench had sampled these small pieces and acquired a taste for them. Then I remembered the dehydrated sliced potatoes we had once used at Wotton lakes in an attempt to attract carp into one of our swims. Some days later we had caught tench fairly drooling with potato pulp!

So to prove my point I boiled up some big potatoes and cut them into small dice, using some for groundbait and the remainder for hookbaits. I was right! The tench loved them and, more important of course, my hookbaits remained immune from the attentions of the ever hungry hordes of rudd.

I have never tried this experiment on another water but I am quite sure that there must be many places where the situation and the problems are similar. There I am sure it would be equally effective.

The clay pits taught me much about tench fishing and I hope they will teach me more as time goes by, but one particular lesson comes to mind and I record it as a warning to those who have a particular enthusiasm for restocking and introducing new tench 'blood' into a small water. I cannot say 'Do not do so,' for that would probably be wrong of me. What I will say is 'Think hard before you do.'

Some years ago one of the club members transferred a number of tench from a big fertile water to the clay pits. For a time we were blessed with four-pound tench, but as the season wore on those big tench grew leaner and hungrier until they became all-head-and-no-body. They were sorry sights and now that they have apparently all died off, I hope I shall never have to witness such pathetic creatures again. The clay-pit tench are only small; one could almost call them a pigmy breed, but they are perfectly shaped, full of fight and very pleasant to behold. Obviously they are as good as they are ever likely to be and I for one would have them no other way.

# 12 The Canal

The Aylesbury arm of the Grand Union canal could hardly be called a reputable tench water, but it held tench and it was conveniently near to my home. I used to fish it regularly for bream, roach and, in the winter, for pike. Chances of catching a bag of tench were almost non-existent, but there were a few dodges we knew in the days when the canal was used extensively by barge traffic. In the process I caught a few accidental tench. One of the dodges was to fish opposite the loading bay near the mill. Wheat was one of the many cargoes carried by the barges and inevitably much grain was discharged into the water on unloading days. It was very understandable, therefore, that many fish, mostly bream and roach, but including a few tench, accumulated around the loading bay. It was also understandable that they developed a taste for wheat. For a number of years we fished with stewed wheat and caught fish of all three species; later we experimented and learned that soaked wheat was just as effective as that which had been carefully stewed. I was to think about this many years later when I fished at the Mere (see Chapter 14) and found that the tench, bream, roach and rudd there quickly developed a liking for uncooked grain. Not that there was much advantage in it. It was as easy, and indeed much quicker, to cook the wheat than to wait for it to soak. Cooked grain is easier to put on a hook too, but there is undoubtedly an advantage in being able to pre-bait with uncooked grain in waters where fish respond.

I have spent a fair amount of time fishing in the United States, where groundbaiting, or chumming as it is called, is generally illegal, but because carp are regarded as unwanted vermin it is usually overlooked or condoned on carp waters. Perhaps the authorities figure that if shooting spawning carp with bows and arrows is legitimate it would be rather illogical to enforce a 'no groundbait' rule!

So the Americans use corn for carp; and by corn I mean cob corn or maize.

Many waters are overstocked and it cannot be denied that carp can ruin other kinds of fishing if they are allowed to breed undisturbed. That is why resort owners, boat-dock proprietors and the like encourage anglers to fish for carp wherever possible. They often provide barrels of soaked corn at vantage points, and swims known to hold carp, for all and sundry to use.

After a few days in the sun the corn begins to swell and smell. Oh my, how it smells! But there is a sort of unwritten law that every time you pass by the barrel you take a handful of the stuff and throw it in. Then you look for the carbolic soap! There's no doubt about it, however, carp love it and two grains on a no. 6 hook will take them by day or night. It is immune from the attentions of most other fish and one can be fairly sure that any bites come from carp.

There are no tench present in the USA as far as I know, but the American anglers' idea of using soaked corn (or maize as we would call it) to rid waters of carp reminded me of my own canal experiences with soaked wheat. It started a new train of thought and although my early experiments in this country were not immediately successful with tench, they eventually paid off and gave rise to new developments regarding what are now referred to as seed or particle baits.

But let us be sure of one fact. There is nothing new about seed baits. Nor is there anything new in catching fish on cob corn, maize, or tinned sweetcorn.

We first caught tench from our canal on what was then usually referred to as corn-on-the-cob in the 1940s! And we caught fish on barley, rice, beans and green peas (as did our fathers before us).

Seed baits have proved more successful in recent years for the simple reason that, suddenly, anglers have begun to believe in them and fish them with confidence.

Any grain left to soak for any length of time begins to ferment and smell and despite the fact that we once believed that stewed wheat had to remain sweet and fresh, we have learned since that what smells pretty evil to us, is attractive to tench, carp, bream and other fish.

In our early days, fishing the canal, it was not an uncommon practice to use brewers' grains for groundbait. We had a local brewery nearby at that time and they were not too difficult to acquire. Those who have used them will know of their peculiar smell – a sour, fermenting smell not at all unlike soaked wheat or maize. So, if that

A recent tench from a corn-baited swim

kind of groundbait was good enough for our grandfathers, why should not fermenting grain be good enough for us?

It is not easy to accept the fact that tench and carp will readily take *hard* baits. We have striven to make our pastes soft and our cooked baits tender, because we've believed it the right thing to do. And yet, as I have mentioned before, tench will eat snails (shells and all) until they fairly rattle. Why should they not take hard maize if they are attracted to it? They took hard wheat when we fished the canal *and* occasionally they took a grain of seed from a corn cob. Strictly speaking that *is* maize. The only difference is that the Indian maize we know is as hard as a rock and does not soften very noticeably in water. It ferments and it smells to high heaven but it never really softens. Tench find it attractive and I have, in recent years, caught them full of it after pre-baiting a swim heavily with it.

I will have more to say about seed baits later; I mention maize briefly here because of the common factors involved in our old style canal fishing and our latest developments in this field. There is nothing new in fishing!

Readers may be interested enough to try something about which Chicago outdoorsman and broadcaster Art Mercier told me. It was, he said, unnecessary to soak the corn after the first few days, and he further told me that it wasn't even necessary to soak the hookbait! I did not believe what he told me at first. I felt sure it was one gigantic leg-pull, but I can assure you that it really works for carp out there.

What you do is this. After a couple of days' feeding with soaked corn you begin to throw it in unsoaked and let it swell up naturally on the lake bottom. To begin with, the carp take the soaked corn, then they wait for the dry stuff to swell up before eating it. Any hard grains are left for another day to soften up a little, but eventually the carp become 'hooked on the hard stuff'. They eat it as quickly as it is thrown in! It is no longer necessary to use soft hookbaits! You drill a hole in a couple of corn grains and hang them on your hook! And because they're hard, and because the carp have become accustomed to taking hard grains, they are not even suspicious about feeling the hook!

I have my doubts as to whether our carp would fall for such tactics, but I believe there is a chance that the tench might.

If a tench can swim around happily with its stomach crammed to bursting point with hard-shelled water snails, I see no reason why it should not be just as happy with a feed of hard maize. I am quite sure the maize would be easier to digest!

Today the canal has changed. Few boats or barges use it, and it is overgrown and heavily silted. But it still holds tench and outside the town it takes on a great deal more character. It bends and twists and I am reminded of the days when heavy boat traffic eroded the banks and kept a deep channel clear through the middle. Those eroded banks were once the scene of some very interesting fishing. In them could be found a small olive-green worm, and at times this proved to be an excellent tench bait. It was a very insignificant-looking worm (I'm sure it *has* a name, but I do not know what it is) but when the barge traffic was on the move, the tench would take it seemingly in preference to any other bait. It was the recognized practice in those days, every time a barge came through, for the anglers along the banks of the canal to grumble. It was the done thing; and while I sometimes grumbled just to conform, I was secretly glad to see the barges approach. Very often I caught a tench on my little olive-green worms a few moments after one had passed!

Some years after World War Two, match fishing became popular along the canal with the result that maggots were used in large quantities. As the water became more and more silted and weed-choked the fish became much more difficult to catch, but I found that by using very small hooks, fine links and single maggot baits I could extract the odd tench from the diminishing clear holes. Eventually these holes in the weeds became so small that it was difficult to drop a bait and float in them. It was then that I learned the advantage of an even larger rod than I had used previously. I had a fourteen footer made of Spanish reed. Its action was all tip, and it had little power, but I was able to *lower* my tackle into the small clearings in the weed. This was about the finest I ever fished for tench, and it is, perhaps, just as well that the fish I caught were small.

I used a tiny 'toothpick' float of porcupine quill, cocked by one tiny dust shot. My line was never more than 2 lb breaking-strain, and my hook size was no. 16. Those tench hardly moved the float at all, and I cannot remember a bite which took it right under, but by striking very quickly I caught a fair number of small fish. I rarely caught more than one at a sitting and if I ever caught two tench averaging a pound, I considered I had done well. Despite the stiffness of my reed rod, I was able, by keeping over the fish, to tire it without it becoming unduly weeded.

Today, although I do not fish the canal regularly, I still tend to use a long rod and 'drop into' my swim.

I have a modern match rod which is vastly different from my original old reed, but though it is less likely to be broken I doubt if it has any great advantage for what is a relatively light-hearted kind of fishing.

I have learned a few wrinkles since my early days, however, and one in particular, which was passed on to me by Billy Lane, is worth recording here because it *does* work occasionally in this and other canals.

It's a matchman's idea, and not aimed at catching tench. In fact it catches roach and rudd much more frequently, but where tench are holed up in small shoals it can be extremely effective. Cloud bait, which has little food value, is introduced in very small quantities at frequent intervals and the tiny toothpick float tackle is dropped into the cloud. The hook, a no. 16, is baited with a minute piece of paste no larger than a pin's head and allowed to sink slowly through the cloud. This tiny bait portion is literally 'balanced' on the very point of the hook but despite its size it is obviously regarded as a plum piece sinking in a misty cloud of nothingness. Billy, as I recall, used the idea to master some particularly difficult canal roach. He may like to know that it has accounted for a few tench as well.

I cannot claim to have caught a big tench from the canal, nor can I claim to have discovered anything revolutionary from fishing it. But I did learn that there were plenty of fish under my own bank and that it was possible to catch them. This largely came about because of what an uncle of mine once said to me. After watching me casting well past the middle of the canal he said 'Why don't you walk down to the next lock, cross over, walk back up and fish on the opposite bank?'

When I asked him why I should do this, he replied 'Because that's what you've spent all morning trying to do from here; you'll find it easier from there!' Profound words; and some I have never forgotten.

# 13 Castle Lake

Throughout this book, and indeed throughout my fishing life I have always been reluctant to accept as gospel all the general 'rules' of tench fishing. I have made it quite clear in earlier chapters that traditional tench-fishing methods did not always seem to offer me the best chance of catching fish and that, wherever possible, I tried to apply my fishing methods to suit the circumstances.

I have explained, for instance, that, in order to deal with a number of situations where tench were not biting boldly, I applied the lift method successfully. This was a breakaway from tradition and it was the correct thing to do in the circumstances; but in many respects it caused confusion among anglers who were, perhaps, new to tench fishing. What happened in effect was that one set of rules was scrapped and a new set accepted!

Because of its success in some situations, the lift method became regarded as the method for all tench fishing, which was a sad mistake. I had no wish for this to come about, nor did I at any time suggest that traditional methods should be forgotten or ignored. I merely stated that, very often, it was advisable to break the rules and try something different, but the lift method became so popular that instead of being used to deal with special situations it was put to use a great deal more than it need have been. It became the rule rather than the exception. And I cannot believe that rules, as such, are good for any form of fishing.

What a lot of anglers failed to recognize was the fact that there *are* waters where the lift method does not work. There are waters, too, where some other, unusual technique is better than any of the accepted methods traditional or otherwise.

Castle Lake was a water which never, to the best of my knowledge, responded to lift fishing. It held large numbers of good quality tench and for the greater part of the time, simple tackle was all that was required to catch them. This tackle was baited with ordinary bread paste and adjusted so that the float lay at half-cock while a foot or more of line separated the bottom shot from the hook. Back to the traditional rig in fact. I knew from what other anglers of experience had told me, that the lift method simply would not work here. I could *not* understand why, and to this day I can offer no explanation, but I did not waste time trying to prove any point. I fished with orthodox rigs and caught my share of tench, but I was not happy because I was quite sure that there were times when tench were feeding and I was not catching as many as I should!

Castle Lake, big and comparatively shallow, with an uneven bottom of soft mud for the greater part of it, was very weedy. Like all good tench lakes it had to be worked on if results were to be achieved. Swims had to be cleared and dragged from the bank and while a few of the very deep holes out in the middle were weed-free they produced fewer tench to boat anglers than those shallower ones which had been cleared. The tench responded to groundbaiting and pre-baiting and when they were 'on' it needed little in the way of skill to hook them. Sound tackle and a knowledge of how to handle it were, however, essential, for the fish were strong dour fighters. All of which tells the reader very little.

There were problems at Castle Lake, however, which did not exist on any other water I fished. There was no possibility of fishing during the night or the early morning. The earliest I could hope to commence fishing was about eight o'clock in the morning and I was never really happy about making such a late start. I felt that I had missed the best of the fishing before I wetted a line and, as I had to leave before dusk, I was quite convinced that I was going home just when I should have been arriving. Thinking back on my experiences of evening tench fishing now, I doubt if I would have achieved a great deal even if I had been allowed to stay later, but I did not think so at the time.

Making the most of the daytime tench fishing, as I had to at Castle Lake, found me trying some of my old tricks to tempt the sometimes unenthusiastic tench. I tried fishing in the margins with slowly sinking baits with little success and I crept around the shallows trying to spot and stalk fish on bright sunny days. I caught a few in the margins but I remember only once succeeding in the extreme shallows. That day I caught two tench in quick succession on lob-worms. I threw directly into their path and twitched the baits gently as each tench approached. It worked both times, but it has not done so since.

The unorthodox did eventually pay off, however, and in later seasons I had a lot of fun with tench caught from boat swims, as I will describe later. Meanwhile, like the bank swims, some of the boat swims had to be cleared of weed. This meant a lot of hard work with heavy drags throughout the season. Small throwing drags were useful to clear lightly weeded swims, but to get to grips with the thick weed proper, it was essential to use a heavy-duty job. There was no question of throwing it, it was much too heavy.

Other friends helped, of course, and we found that one of the best ways of clearing a swim was to seesaw the big drag back and forth through the area until it came back clean. We attached the drag to the middle of the long rope instead of at one end, and by drawing it back and forth between two fixed points, a hard and dirty job was made a little easier. But it was always a difficult task, as some of us had already learned at Wotton years previously.

Sometimes we would work from bank to boat; at other times we would work from two boats, and here is where we met trouble. It is absolutely essential for both boats to be firmly *staked*, not just anchored, otherwise the pull on the drag will simply tow the boat. We drove big stakes into the mud at four points around each boat and lashed them all securely. The drag was cleared at each boat after each pull, and the weed dropped back into the water. Some of it drifted away, but most of it sank to the bottom and remained there.

The boats on Castle Lake were flat-bottomed punts, equipped with good anchors and chains that rattled enough to scare the living daylights out of any fish within three miles! I never liked them and never used them. I have a 'thing' about anchored boats, noisy or otherwise, and about the only time I would ever fish from one is if I was absolutely alone. Then, any movement of the boat which upsets my delicately balanced float tackle can only be caused by me! With the best will in the world two anglers cannot float fish properly from a boat that is merely anchored. When one of them moves, the other's float goes under or lies flat and as the day goes on each is convinced that the other is deliberately spoiling his chances! Some beautiful friendships have ended that way.

Waiting for the bite . . .

. . . and netting the tench at Castle Lake

I would much prefer to fish from the bank, but I cannot deny that I have caught many hundreds of tench from boats. The boats Ken, Joe and I fished from, however, were always as firmly staked for fishing as they were for dragging operations. Apart from a few deep holes, Castle Lake was not very deep and the big sapling stakes we cut for holding the boat still while we dragged were also used for holding it still while we fished. They were driven into the soft mud very close to the boat at each 'corner' so that the boat was literally wedged tightly between them. They were then lashed firmly to fittings on the side of the boat with strong ropes. As an added precaution the tops of the poles, which were now protruding about eight feet out of the water, were bent inwards to meet each other fore and aft, and these were then lashed together to form an arch over each end of the boat. The boat then became a stable platform, and apart from tightening the ropes occasionally as the poles settled, no other maintenance was necessary.

Of course, there could never be any disagreement over choice of swim. Once our spot was chosen we stayed there until we stopped fishing. The job of securing the boat took too long to be treated lightly, and we paid so much attention to our choice of swim for this very reason that we were never, to the best of my recollection, mistaken. By staying put and working at different methods we invariably caught fish sooner or later.

I still feel that hire boats, especially those in shallow soft-bottomed lakes, would be better if supplied with four strong sapling poles instead of their inevitable rusty anchor chains!

In deeper waters, and waters with hard bottoms, it is not practicable to use poles, of course, but a point worth remembering is that a boat will remain more stable if *all* the anchor chain is paid out. If two anchors are available, so much the better. Boats drift badly on tight anchors, but allowances must be made, of course, to position a boat when a long anchor chain is used. This is just a question of experience, however, and can soon be mastered.

Fishing into the wind from a boat is not easy, and the temptation to anchor so that a lee is formed in front of it, with the wind blowing from behind, is very great. There is nothing to be said against it as a rule, but when the sun is strong and the wind is rippling the surface of the water, it is advisable to pay particular attention to the sun's direction. It is virtually impossible to fish directly into the sun, as I found out very often at Castle Lake. The surface of the water was seldom really calm and the glittering 'water diamonds' reflected by the sun made life unbearable unless the boat was properly positioned so as to avoid the direct rays. By changing floats and adjusting tackle, almost any wind situation could be dealt with; but it was never possible to blot out the sun! Polaroid spectacles helped, of course, but the sun shone mostly on those days when I had left mine behind.

In my opinion, fishing punts are just about the most uncomfortable contraptions ever created. There is nothing in this world worse for the morale than to be perched on, or straddled across, a narrow boat thwart; and as fishing is to be enjoyed rather than endured, it is advisable to take some form of cushion whenever such boats are used. In the days when we fished Castle Lake I found a piece of thick foam rubber to be well worth the room it took up in my tackle bag. Later, some inflatable plastic cushions became available, and while they lasted they were extremely good. Their life, however, was short and they were very unreliable.

Richard Walker, in later years, came up with a much better proposition. A lightly inflated, small rubber inner tube such as is used on heavy duty motor mowers can be used with or without some form of canvas 'cushion cover'. Mine goes with me now every time I think I might be using a boat. I would not be without it.

For sheer comfort, however, and especially when it is intended to stay for a long time anchored or staked firmly in one spot, I am still of the opinion that the common wooden deckchair is unsurpassable. Surprisingly, I have never yet found a fishing punt that is too narrow to allow for the setting up of a deckchair while leaving ample room for me to sit on it comfortably. I have spent days and nights at a time with a deckchair as my only means of sitting, fishing and sleeping. Night fishing was not allowed at Castle Lake, but I spent many long and lazy days there, fishing from my deckchair.

When I first fished from a boat, I was already brainwashed into believing that short rods were essential, but the more I fished, the more I realized that this simply was not true. I have tried them all from six feet upwards and I am convinced that a rod of eleven or twelve feet is much more suitable for striking and handling a fish from a boat.

At Castle Lake I used a built-cane eleven footer. It was referred to in those days as an 'Avon type', and very nice it was too. I still have it and use it, though my hollow-glass version of it is much lighter and just as effective. Somehow, though, it does not have the same sweetness of feel about it as my older rod. Perhaps I'm sentimental, but I am still very fond of my old built cane rods and I cannot forget the pleasure they gave me in those early days.

A longer rod also has the advantage over a short poker in that a hooked tench, heading for the underside of the boat, can be bullied out a lot easier. I have heard many stories of tench wrapping the line round the anchor chain and smashing the tackle, but I can only remember it happening to me once. Then I was using a very short rod and I had no control over the fish whatsoever. I am happy with a longer rod, whether I am fishing from bank or boat, but I believe that rod length is really a matter of individual taste.

I have, for example, in recent years found extreme pleasure in using a soft actioned ultra-light nine footer which came about as a result of experiments involving the development of a touch leger rod. It so happens that this delightful little tool serves as an excellent float rod in water no deeper than six feet. It becomes unwieldy if the water is much deeper, but its extreme lightness and casting power make it a useful rod for fishing a sliding float rig. It is not a long-range float rod, but it can be used to leger at extreme range.

The fishing at Castle Lake was interesting because it could not be approached in the truly orthodox manner. Dawn sessions in shallow swims for instance were out, as I have already explained, and it was necessary to make the most of every daylight hour. This, of course, had some bearing upon the choice of swim.

I remember having written, several years previously, the following words:

> Choice of swim is very important, and depends entirely upon what you wish to get out of it. Do you want a couple of hours fast fishing followed by twelve hours when the swim is completely dead? If so, choose the shallower, four to five feet swim and groundbait it liberally before fishing it at crack of dawn.
>
> Or do you want to pick up the odd tench every now and then all through the day, even though the early morning fishing produces little or nothing? If so, choose a swim some nine or ten feet deep and stick to it all day.
>
> In either case I would hazard that the numbers of tench caught over a period would be about equal.

I was referring to what I regarded as typical tench lakes at the time and, from my own experiences before and since I wrote it, I think the advice is still fairly sound.

Certainly at Castle Lake it applied. Shallow boat swims were not very productive later in the season, and it was easy to convince oneself that the tench had done all their feeding in the early hours before the anglers had arrived. Occasionally they could be encouraged back to life for a while by using a throwing drag. Sometimes a good stirring up of the bottom mud would bring tench into the area to investigate, but groundbait seldom had the desired effect. My first move on arrival at a shallow swim that had already been previously cleared of weed was to rake the bottom for ten minutes or so before fishing. It worked often enough to convince me that it was worth the effort, but the more I fished Castle Lake the more I realized that I had to concentrate on the holes that were over eight feet and no more than twelve feet in depth.

These holes needed clearing, too, but they were not as heavily weeded as the shallower swims. I found that I could then often catch tench throughout the day at a rate that kept me interested. It was here that I learned a little more about unorthodox fishing, and the conditions in which certain methods worked best.

Traditional laying-on methods with regular baits were productive enough, and most anglers there were content to cast out their tackle and sit back to await the tench's pleasure; but to me it seemed an interminable time between bites. I was convinced, as I mentioned at the very beginning of this chapter, that there were more tench about than there at first appeared to be, and that only a percentage of them would eventually fall to stationary bottom-fished baits. So I began to experiment. Knowing that a tench will sometimes take a bait almost as soon as it hits the bottom, I began to cast regularly and frequently instead of watching a motionless float for hours at a time. It paid off more often than not, and it soon became common practice for Ken and me to wind in and re-cast every few minutes. Local anglers, fishing in the accepted style, regarded us as impatient; told us we were flogging ourselves to death; informed us that we ought to know well enough that tench came along in their own sweet time and not before; but failed completely to realize that we were catching about three times the number of tench that they were!

In the course of this somewhat offbeat way of tench fishing, it became obvious that some of the tench were taking the bait before it reached the bottom, and, remembering our experiences with the slowly sinking baits in the margins at Wotton, we rigged up tackles to make the baits sink more slowly. There seemed to be no real explanation why these tench, supposedly confirmed bottom feeders, should decide to take baits at mid-water. In the margins at Wotton it could probably be explained; here there seemed no logical reason for their behaviour. It was noticeable, however, that it happened mostly when the weather was warm but the sky overcast. I believe it will pay any tench angler to try a slowly sinking bait under a self-cocking float when these conditions prevail and a bottom-fished bait is being completely ignored. It is a simple matter to slide the cocking shot or shots up to the float so that the bait sinks slowly under its own weight.

Unlike the moving baits used in the marginal rushes, baits fished in the milfoil-fringed open holes need not be small.

There is sometimes a case for using maggots both as hookbaits and free offerings, but generally speaking, I have found lobworms to be the best bait in these circumstances.

Undoubtedly, despite general opinion, there are situations where a moving bait, and one which is definitely *not* on the bottom, is more acceptable to the tench than one which lies still. Perhaps there is a special attraction about a moving bait; perhaps some tench have learned to view a stationary bait with suspicion; perhaps there is less *time* to inspect a moving bait. Who knows?

Many times at Castle Lake Ken and I took tench on baits fished only a foot or so below the surface. They were allowed to drift slowly around the swim, covering a wide area, the float moving continually under the influence of the slightest breeze. Most of the bites came when the bait had drifted close to the soft weed that surrounded the swim, but they were liable to come anywhere and at any time during the day.

I have never known tench behave this way except in very warm weather, and even then, *not* when the sun has been shining brightly. I have often wondered if certain foods are released from the bottom to remain in suspension at mid-water or near to the surface after a particularly vigorous digging session by the tench earlier; but I hardly think that tench would then be looking for food items as big as lobworms.

It has been suggested to me that tench sometimes seek the surface layer of water because it is warmer than that below. I am sure that they do, but, generally speaking, I believe they do so to bask rather than to feed. Whatever the explanation, and I'm sure we shall never know the real answer, I ask readers to believe me when I say that

A tench from the thick weeds at Castle Lake

you can catch tench from *some* waters on baits fished well off the bottom. I suggest they try it again and again when other methods are proving non-productive, and that if they are reluctant to interfere with their regular bottom-fished baits, they set up a spare outfit and experiment.

Although these particular moving baits did not produce results in bright sunshine, we later found a method of presenting them that did. There was a deep and fairly weed-free hole in the middle of Castle Lake which had a hard gravel bottom. It was a good tench hole in the autumn and a fairly reliable daytime tench spot in high summer. By the end of August, however, tench fishing was, to all intents and purposes, over, and by mid-September, most anglers were already thinking in terms of pike fishing. Ken and I fished for perch then and it was in this gravel-bottomed hole that we learned more about tench baits on the move.

Fishing with small red worms on a floatless tackle, and using a small, bored bullet for a casting weight, we developed a style of fishing which paid handsome dividends from late August until the end of September.

We anchored the boat well away from the deep hole, using the soft weed beds nearby as cover, and made long casts to the far side. After letting the tackle sink we retrieved it with a sink-and-draw action which proved to be deadly for perch. But, quite unexpectedly, we began to catch tench also. Occasionally the bites came when the bait was still sinking, more often they came while it was being retrieved, and this became an exciting late-season method.

True, we caught many more perch than tench, and occasionally we caught big rudd, but every so often the rod would bend slowly and quite decisively towards the water as a big tench hung on to the bait. It only happened, as far as I can remember, when the sun was shining brightly in the middle of the day, but it happened often enough for us to practise the technique regularly and with a fair chance of success.

# 14 The Mere

The first fish I ever caught from the mere was a tench weighing five pounds six ounces! I sat on the boathouse steps, cast a lobworm out into the darkness and held on to the rod. It was only a matter of minutes before I felt a pull and my immediate strike put me into the fish. It was strong and, like a lot of other tench I have hooked at night, it made a long run away from me out into the lake, but as I was using a fairly powerful hollow-glass rod and substantial tackle, it was soon subdued. I remember thinking at the time that this was going to be too easy! How little I knew of the tench in the mere!

Dick Walker and I were just beginning a three-day stint at the mere after receiving a special invitation from the owners to do so. We had been allowed to visit the water in advance, to clear a swim and to pre-bait it fairly thoroughly with Pomenteg groundbait, mashed bread and worms. It was dark when we arrived to fish and, as our swim could only be reached by boat, we decided to leave the serious fishing until the morning. On the boathouse steps we were merely passing the time in a lighthearted fashion until the dawn came, but I confess that I became very excited there and then about our prospects. If fish like this could be caught without preparation or groundbait, what would our baited swim produce next day? In fact, although it produced a number of tench over the next few days it did not produce another five pounder. Nor did we take another tench from the boathouse steps!

That visit, however, though the only one we were allowed that season, was the forerunner of many visits during the next few years. It was a visit of reconnaissance, of studying the depth and contours of the mere and of trying to figure out where the tench might be and why. Despite appalling weather we had good morning and evening sessions with the tench, but our attempts at night fishing were both washouts – literally! We caught excellent rudd and perch,

A typical tench from the mere

a few eels, several accidental pike and just over a score of tench. Not an outstanding catch as far as tench were concerned, but satisfactory enough for our first visit.

The following year we were allowed to go again and this time Ken accompanied us. We chose a swim much nearer to the boathouse and baited it liberally in advance with the mixture much the same as before. This time, however, we introduced several sacks of brandlings as well as the bait and lobworms.

The swim itself was fringed at both ends with reedmace; the bottom, though silted over with rotting leaves and vegetation, was basically hard. It shelved up steeply towards the bank from a depth of ten feet a rod's length out to about two feet close in. Because of our limited time we commenced fishing at midnight on 16 June and Dick, for some reason best known to himself, chose to fish with a long antenna float illuminated by a torch beam.

Dick and I had used this method many times before for roach but never, to the best of my knowledge, for tench.

Details of the catch have been recorded elsewhere so I will not repeat them except to say that Dick caught twenty-one tench close

Ken Taylor lands a lively mere tench

to the rushes at one end of the swim while Ken and I, using simple leger tackle caught about ten each at the other end. Ken and I stayed on for another day after Dick had left and added another dozen or so to our score, but there were no outstanding fish caught.

Discussing the situation later we came to the conclusion that, although rushes fringed the swim at both ends, the big acreage of dense rushes at the right hand end, where Dick had chosen to fish, probably held a great many more tench than the thin patch at the left hand end where Ken and I had been seated. Most of Dick's tench had been taken very close to the rush stems and it made sense to us to try and tempt them out into the open next time we fished.

We had also begun to take an interest in the big bream we had seen in the vicinity and we thought that an extra heavy groundbaiting, with trails leading from the pockets and clear patches in the rushes into the cleared swim might attract them also.

Sometimes it did. Sometimes not. Our catches were strangely inconsistent and there were times when we failed to catch a fish of any kind at all by day or by night.

I have, however, lost count of the number of big bream we have caught from that one swim and I think I could guarantee to catch a seven pounder given just two days to fish! But we are not concerned with bream here. I mentioned them because at times they have been mixed in with a bag of tench and only one noticeable fact has really come to light during the whole of the time we have fished the mere. It is this.

The more bread and/or groundbait we introduce into the swim, the greater becomes the likelihood of catching bream instead of tench. Bread and meal groundbaits do of course attract tench, but at the mere worms, brandlings and maggots seem generally more effective. Blood and meal groundbaits attract both tench and bream, but they attract even more eels, which can be very exasperating at night.

Our experiences over the years have caused us to believe that our chosen swim, although very productive at times, does not have the right kind of bottom to harbour large numbers of tench. For this reason we decided one season to fish from the boat in the thick rush beds. We first of all did some extensive swim clearing, for although there were deep pockets completely free from rush growth, much of the area was covered with that tough weed, *potamageton natans*, often referred to as 'tench weed'.

We swam around in the biggest of the nearby pockets after forcing the boat through the thicket and anchoring it firmly. The bottom was hard but covered with a thin layer of rotted vegetation. Here and there we located coils of rusty wire and other hazards which, though falling to pieces with age, would certainly not have helped matters had they been allowed to remain! We pulled up the tough weed by hand, we trimmed off the overhanging broken rush stems and we generally made sure that the swim was weed and snag free. It was a long narrow swim, completely surrounded on all sides by rushes and demanding very accurate casting from the anchored boat, but it had one big advantage. It was sheltered from the wind. This big exposed mere is subject to more than its fair share of wind and at times the waves can be as high as to make fishing extremely difficult if not quite impossible. In the shelter of the bay, as we quickly learned to call it, we were able to fish completely untroubled by wind. The tall rushes acted as a complete windbreak and we were able to use delicate lift floats on an almost glassy surface irrespective of conditions out in the main part of the mere.

It proved an interesting experiment inasmuch as we caught quite a lot of tench, bream and rudd during the daytime, but there seemed not to be any particular pattern regarding the feeding behaviour of any of the fish.

Sometimes the area would be full of rudd feeding madly at all depths with no sign of a tench being present. Sometimes, using simple lift tackle we would catch tench after tench during short exciting sessions. Sometimes we could only catch bream and on all too many occasions we could catch nothing at all!

It was not unusual, however, to see tench rolling and surfacing on the edge of the rush bed, especially if we had allowed some loose surface crusts to float there. I am convinced that the crust *attracted* the tench, but at no time did I ever see a tench take, or attempt to take, a surface crust from that swim. But on the opposite side of the mere, a long, long, haul away, I had a different experience one hot day when there was very little doing in the usual tench swim. I took the boat across the wide expanse of clear water to a point where the margin was partly shaded by the branches of a big elm tree (which has long since died of the so-called Dutch elm disease). There was some slight activity right on the edge where the sunlight met the shadow. The rushes trembled and swayed as fish worked between the stems and we wondered if it might be one of those days when the tench were feeding in shelter. It's always an interesting exercise to try and tempt, coax, or bully them out of the thicket, but it isn't always easy to hook them when the surface is unrippled and the sun throws shadows on to the water in advance of your coming. Normally tench don't seem to worry too much about a bit of boat noise and, while it's always advisable not to do a clog dance over a baited swim, the dropping of a bait box (which sounds like distant thunder in the quiet of the early morning) doesn't seem to deter them too much. I remember once fishing with a dear old friend who kept knocking his pipe on the side of the punt. I cringed every time he did it but we still caught over forty tench, so from then on I figured it didn't make too much difference! Tench in the shallow margins, however, are very easily scared, despite the fact that they are under cover, and I've known all activity cease the moment an oar has rattled in the rowlock.

Today the oars were tucked away in the bottom of the boat and I was using the little electric trolling motor which is almost completely noiseless. When I reached a spot within casting range of the margin, I lowered the anchors carefully and quietly.

I didn't cast right away, but sat and watched for a while trying to figure out what fish were moving. They could have been rudd, tench or even bream, but as all the activity was below the surface I couldn't tell.

There was no attack on the crusts at all so I fixed up a zoomer float tackle and baited with a lob tail. I like to use small red worms for margin-feeding tench but today I had nothing but lobs. They had recently made a round trip of about 1600 miles in the car boot, without severe loss, but they were undoubtedly nearing the end of their time! I filled a bait box with chopped-up portions, and scattered them well into and around the margin with a catapult. They made an almost noiseless entry and the fish didn't appear to be scared by them – which, at that stage, was important. It's easy enough to pack chopped worms into a ball of groundbait in order to throw them out, and in a regular swim this would have been the proper procedure, but in the shallow margins it doesn't work that way. The object of groundbaiting in an open swim is to draw fish to you, but when you know where the fish are it's pointless pounding the area with heavy stodge. It is, however, necessary to start the fish foraging, or alternatively, to wean them over from whatever they're eating to the hook bait you're going to use. And if you can do that without creating a disturbance you're in with a chance.

My experience in the past has been that if I take the boat to within hand throwing distance (chopped worms or loose maggots can only be thrown a limited distance by hand) I scare the fish. It may be the hand waving and the shadows caused by it, or it may be that the rocking of the boat sends warning signals towards the fish, but whatever the reason, I'm never happy if I have to approach too closely. I'm sold on long range fishing in these circumstances and even then I feel I make more noise than I'd like to.

The zoomer is not the easiest of floats to cast without disturbance, but at least its weight is concentrated and if you 'feather' the line at the extent of the cast you can put it down gently most times.

I started off by fishing a foot or so away from the edge of the reeds. Those first few casts were 'ranging shots' really; I didn't want to get caught up in the thicket early on in the proceedings. That's *all* you need to ruin this kind of fishing completely.

I gradually eased forward until I was fishing with my float touching the rushes, and I began to catch fish right away. They were rudd, however, not tench, and in view of their complete disregard of the loose crusts, which were still floating around, I was puzzled. Not that it mattered, of course. I like to catch rudd in the middle of the day and it doesn't bother me too much how I catch them. I suppose I had seven or eight before they stopped biting and, although they weren't really big fish, some of them topped the pound – which is nice fishing in my book.

A slurping noise to the left made me look up and I noticed that one of the pieces of crust had disappeared. There was a swirl and a hint of greeny-bronze in the middle of the rush bed as a tench rolled over another piece and broke it into a million fragments. Whether it meant to do just that, of course, is a matter for conjecture, but I've seen carp do it many times before and I've watched helplessly while the dislodged fragments were sucked in like porridge while they sank.

I couldn't see what was happening below the surface but I took off my float and sent a piece of dunked crust into the area where it was all happening. It had barely hit the water before it disappeared and the line tightened so quickly that I had no need to strike. It wasn't a big fish, but even a three pound tench can be fun in those circumstances. To take such a fish from the top was something rather special.

A mixed bag of tench and rudd

It was a strange day really. I had caught rudd using tench tactics and now a tench on what was essentially a rudd or carp presentation. Several more followed and it was the very fact that these fish were behaving differently that made it so enjoyable.

It all ended when a great brute of a pike threw itself at a bait being wound back to the boat. It leapt clear of the water, landed with an almighty splosh back in the rushes, changed direction and put paid to any more surface tench fishing that day!

Catching tench alone gives me great pleasure; catching them by a new method or on a new bait, or following some preconceived plan, gives me even more. My ultimate tench-fishing enjoyment, however, comes from sharing my pleasure with someone else. I have done it many times at Wotton and other waters, and I have especially delighted in the look of rapture on a novice angler's face when he has netted and is now fondly admiring his first big tench.

Opportunity to do this sort of thing does not come often at the mere. There the situation is different from other waters I fish, but on one occasion Ken and I were privileged to take Ian Howcroft, a young friend and very capable angler, to the water.

We were not intending to fish much at all that weekend. It was fine and warm and it seemed like a good time to swim around and try and find out a bit more about the mere. The water was invitingly warm and with cold drinks in the 'chatties' (earthenware pots which I had recently brought back from Egypt, and which keep liquids ice-cold when left out in the hot sun), and deckchairs on the boat-house staging, we looked forward to spending most of the time in swimming trunks; but we had to look after Ian first. This was his weekend really, and he was anxious to start fishing for the tench and bream. He really wanted to catch a six pound bream and he thought that if he could use the boat and fish all night (something Ken and I had never got round to doing) he might well stand a chance. We thought so, too, and we decided to let him fish in the bay. We swam around in it for a time, checked it for weed and snags and generally muddied it up for him. Then, towards evening, we took him out in the boat, anchored it firmly, baited up with a mixture of bread, multi-meal groundbait, maggots and brandlings, and left him to it!

Ian worked hard in that swim, and all told he extracted fourteen good tench and three bream from it. The best two bream were five and a half pounds and six pounds respectively and I don't know who was the more pleased! Make no mistake about it, it was a first-class

Part of Ian's night catch. The bream were not retained

piece of angling on Ian's part and although our efforts on his behalf certainly helped, they would have been wasted on anyone with less angling ability.

How often I wonder does a venture like this come off? How many times have we all tried to pass on some of our angling pleasure to someone else with less opportunity and found that everything has gone wrong? I know my best laid schemes have often gone astray, when I have tried to wave my magic wand for special friends; so it is all the more pleasing when it *does* come off.

I still like catching fish and I hope I always will, but on familiar waters I confess that it gives me more pleasure to see someone else hit the jackpot and achieve an ambition of long standing than it does to catch a sackful myself.

Ken and I had work to do on the other boat that weekend so we got on with that while Ian fished and tried to sleep in the daytime, but we allowed ouselves an hour or two in our favourite rudd swim, where we usually catch good fish right close to the margins. It is an easy and very enjoyable form of fishing requiring no groundbait or preparation; just a float rod, a loaf of bread and a few worms.

Those few hours turned out to be some of the best we have had there. The fish were not quite as big as usual, but we caught over fifty of them on floating crust and float-fished worms. We also saw signs of tench from time to time and we finally went searching for mud in the area. If that sounds strange let me explain.

In the mere there is very *little* mud, but Ken and I felt that if we could find some, it might mean there were more tench present. It is possible, as I have already explained, if both time and a good supply of groundbait are available, to attract tench into any swim no matter what the bottom is like, but this weekend we had very little time and even less groundbait. So we went looking for mud, and we found some in a small area surrounded by soft milfoil and looking remarkably like one of the many tench swims we used to fish at the Sawmills with such fabulous results years ago.

We anchored the boat, slid overboard into the soft weed, and started swimming. Presently the weed began to come adrift from the bottom and float up to the surface. Soon we had a fishable area cleaned. Then we went to work on the mud, stirring it up with our feet until the water was filthy. Not a particularly clean job, and one which called for the carbolic soap afterwards, but not really unpleasant. We have done it many times.

I had never been so enthusiastic over a newly found swim, and when we began to find big swan mussels in the mud, I felt sure we had located a natural tench swim. Those were the first mussels we had ever found in this water and, because of past experience, I was quite confident that tench would be present too.

So it turned out to be. By the time we got back to the swim to fish it was seven o'clock in the evening and, after baiting up with our remaining groundbait, we started fishing about half an hour later. At first we were irritated by rudd and for a time it was quite impossible to get a bait to the bottom. Then they disappeared and we were able to settle in to fish the way we wanted to, with peacock-quill lift rigs. How grand it was to see those white quills lift slowly but purposefully to the bites of the tench when they finally came.

We used small hooks and 3 lb lines and those tench fought like demons. In all we took ten of them. Most were over four pounds; two were an ounce under five. Not a spectacular catch but I cannot remember ever enjoying a short tench-fishing session more.

There have been many times at the mere when it has been obvious that the chances of catching fish in the daytime were very slim. Great white patches of groundbait have lain on the bottom a couple of rod-lengths out, and the unrippled surface of the clear water has shown no sign of fish activity whatsoever. On these occasions, Ken and I have usually decided to fish at night, and although there have been occasions when the groundbait has still remained untouched after a biteless night, generally speaking our tench-fishing sessions have been interesting.

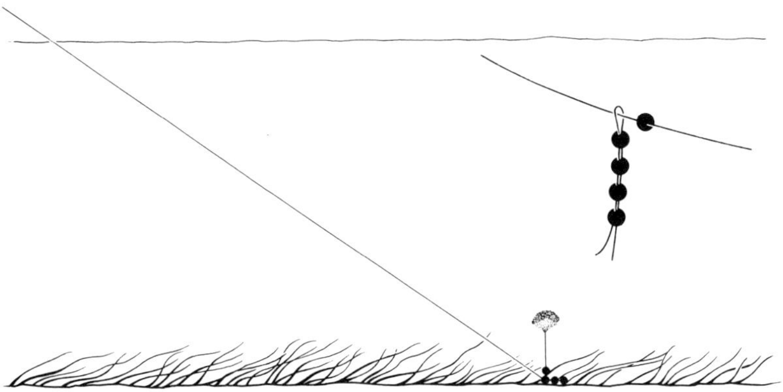

*Figure 6* Legered crust showing useful leger weight made up of swanshots on a nylon link

At the outset we used simple leger tackle with only one fixed shot to hold the bait on the bottom. Later we tried completely leadless tackles and again later we tried sophisticated sliding legers and swivelled swanshot rigs. We tried them all for one reason only. A large number of the bites we had, on baits ranging from lobworms and brandlings to crust cubes, paste and maggots, were seemingly impossible to hit. Our 'glow-bob' indicators would shoot up and hit the rod butts with a healthy crack and our ensuing strike would contact – nothing! Every so often we would hook and land a tench, which encouraged us to think that we were at least on the right track, but our percentage of misses was unbelievable. There was no apparent explanation, and to this day I cannot explain why we missed so many good tench bites in the dark.

Remembering our experiences at the Narrows years ago we tried big baits and bite alarms, and opened the bale-arms of our reels to allow free passage of line. We tried long and short link legers; we tried tight lines and slack lines and we tried fast striking and slow striking without ever once feeling that we had solved the problem. We caught fish, of course, but we missed too many more.

On one memorable night we set our rods in two long rests, so that they poked out about five feet above the water. We then attached 'glow-bob' indicators between the first two rod rings and pulled them down so that they hung suspended only a few inches off the water. Any bites which followed would have to pull the indicator up nearly five feet before it hit the rod butt, and we felt quite sure that some time during that pull there would be a precise and accurate moment at which to strike. We had ten bites that night and we caught eight good tench, a roach and a four pound pike! (Who says pike don't feed at night?)

So here, we thought, was the answer. One hundred per cent success on lobworms, and this particular kind of bite registration seemed to suggest that we had beaten the bogy. All the bites on this occasion, however, were *slow*. There was no hissing of line, and no crack on the rod butt as the bobbin flew up to hit it. We wondered then, if the fact that we had presented our tackle in this fashion had brought about the slow bites, or whether the fish had just happened to bite slowly on that particular night.

It was October then and this was our last night's tench fishing for that season. We could not pursue the matter further until the following June and when that time came we were faced with the same problem all over again. Six weeks later we were no nearer the solution than we were before and we were eventually obliged to conclude that those tench *did* behave a little differently on that October night. Probably because it *was* October. Finally, because we had met with so many blank evening, morning and daytime sessions, and because we were almost assured of bites on most nights, we began to fish almost exclusively at night with illuminated floats in the manner that Dick had fished some years previously. We still missed a few fish, but our percentage of hooked and landed fish increased enormously.

Only when we had bream in the swim did we experience difficulty in timing the strike, and this, I feel sure, was due to the size of the baits we used. Generally speaking they were big and the bream were apt to move the float out of the torch beam without actually pulling it under.

We eventually solved the problem by using very large hooks and 'beacon' floats similar to the one used by Dick Walker earlier. These floats were made by Bill Watson of Hull. They were up to fifteen inches long and had fine antennae made of very thin fibreglass. The red 'beacon' on top was shotted down to water level and the bites, after some preliminaries, were usually registered as slow deliberate lifts.

At about that time Peter Drennan, an Oxford float manufacturer, was developing a 'windbeater' float quite independently. His finished product was almost identical to the Watson beacon float, but being a mass-produced item, it obviously did not have a fifteen inch hand-filed fibreglass antenna! It proved to be a very successful float for many kinds of still water fishing and was an excellent night

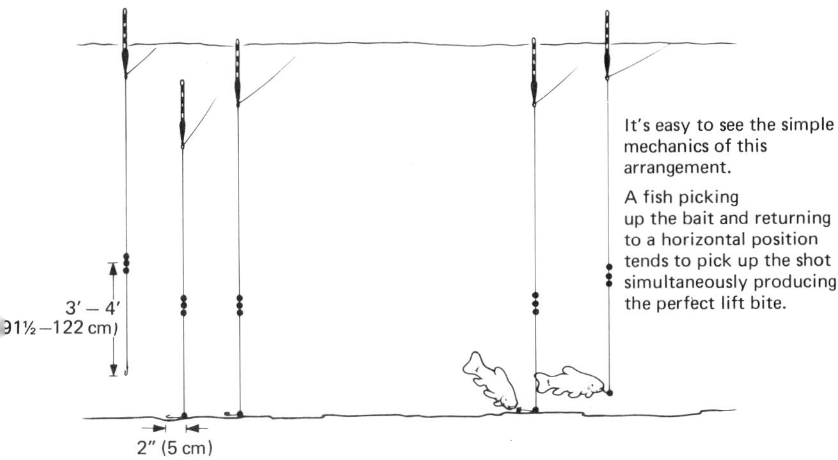


(i) How to set up the windbeater rig. Set the float up with as much of the black and white antenna showing as possible by placing bulk shot about 3 ft 3 ins (1 m) from hook.
(ii) Pinch on single large anchor shot about 2 ins (5 cm) from hook. This shot should be at least heavy enough to sink the rest of the antenna.
(iii) Adjust float so that anchor shot is resting on bottom and sight bob of float is riding on surface.

*Figure 7* Windbeater

float. It has since been superseded by the 'Drift beater' a superb, polystyrene-bodied creation that is even better.

For ordinary situations, however, I have yet to find a float which will show up better or react more positively than a simple lift float made out of peacock quill. It shows up extremely well in the torch beam, and as most bites are of the regular lift-type, the problem of bites which pull the float out of the torch beam, and so confuse the issue, does not often arise.

Night fishing for tench with illuminated floats can be very enjoyable and very productive, but although tench do not seem to be unduly worried about lights, it is as well to remember that they do have small eyes, which may suggest that they do not take kindly to too much light. For this reason, the torch should be fixed so that the beam shines across and not into the water; and once it is set it should be moved as little as possible. Where other anglers are present nearby I believe that it is good manners not to use lights at all. Lights are irritating to other people, and their use could well result in unpleasantness all round! My friends and I only use lights when we are quite sure that there is no possibility of offending others on the water.

One of the advantages of using an illuminated float at night is that it makes one fish properly. By this I mean that the fishing is carried out exactly as it would be by daylight. A cast slightly off target is retrieved and made again, and again if necessary, until the bait is placed, and the float nicely cocked, in what is considered to be the exact spot. A leger, or leadless tackle, cast out in the darkness, could be anywhere from a few inches to a yard or more off target. This would not be acceptable by day; it should not be acceptable by night if it can be avoided. Small baits, much smaller than those used for night-time legering, can be used with illuminated float tackle and although it is by no means always necessary, fish can be struck much more quickly.

There is no pleasure to be gained from pulling tench out on heavy tackle, and while it is quite possible to use fine tackle at night without lights, I am convinced that the illuminated float encourages the use of finer tackle than would normally be used after dark. For some reason, when we fish at night for fish like tench and bream, we all tend to step up our tackle considerably. In pitch darkness this is probably wise. Fine tackle has a nasty habit of becoming snarled up and is much more difficult to handle than the substantial gear and heavier lines generally used by night fishermen.

I developed the rather bad habit of using carp tackle for most of my night fishing back in the early days at Wotton, simply because I felt I had to be insured against the unexpected. Even long after Ken, Joe, and I had stopped fishing seriously for carp, we still fished with carp tackle for most of the time after dark 'just in case'. Having hooked the odd carp by accident on tench tackle I was probably even more cautious than the other two, and this habit stayed with me until I became adept at fishing with an illuminated float at the mere.

Today, in the light of the torch beam, I use the tackle I would normally use by day. My rod is a twelve footer of hollow glass, which was precision made by Hardy's and is a joy to handle in daylight or darkness. It is my first choice of rod for general float fishing for tench by day or night. Used with lines of 3 to 6 lb breaking-strain and hooks varying from no. 14 to no. 6, it casts light and medium float tackle accurately and handles a strong fish extremely well. It strikes quickly enough to deal with the fastest of lift bites, but has an all-through action that allows me to exert just that little bit of extra pressure, which is sometimes needed to deal with a strong fish or a fish obviously heading for a snag or trouble spot. It is also an extremely good boat rod and one which allows me quickly to gain control over a fish hooked at close range or in the confines of a small hole in the weeds. I can keep *over* the fish and steer it out of trouble; *push* it away from me if necessary, and subdue it quickly without ever having to resort to 'violence'.

All in all I have not learned a great deal new at the mere, but some of the finer points of night fishing for tench have come to light during the few years I have fished there. The tench there have responded to some of the better known, and now generally accepted, methods of tench fishing, and I have hopes of experimenting and developing new ideas as time goes by, for the mere is a water which lends itself to experiment.

It has produced a few big tench and it has been the scene of some exciting captures. Ken and I have taken many bream in excess of seven pounds, and on one memorable morning Ken caught a six pound tench within minutes of my landing an eight pound bream. They came in the middle of the day when they were least expected.

It took me years, but I finally achieved a lifelong ambition at the mere. I took my first six pound tench after being within an ounce of that figure many times. Ken took a seven pounder while I was in the USA one season. He took it from the identical spot where I had

Author displays his first 6-pounder (6 lb 2 oz) from the mere

once hooked, by accident, an enormous tench on a portion of dead fish. We estimated it at seven pounds after it escaped and Ken is convinced that it was the same fish. We shall never know of course.

That is another of the pleasures which come from fishing the mere; the uncertainty of it! The greatest pleasure of all, however, comes not from the big fish or the uncertainties but from the very ordinary fish, those tench averaging from three to five pounds, which come to the baited swim and bubble in the early morning sunshine. Those fish which cause us to sit, hands poised above long rods, watching the motionless peacock quills a few yards out. Watching, but not moving, until they begin slowly to lift up out of the oily surface. . . .

# 15 River Tench

I make no bones about it. Most of the tench I have caught from rivers have been accidental catches which just happened along when I was fishing for something entirely different.

Nearly all the waters described so far in this book have been enclosed and quite still, the exceptions being the Canal, the Middle Lake and the Waterfall. These first two have been treated as still waters despite the fact that there is an appreciable flow at times, and the Waterfall is the only one that is truly part of a river system. The methods used to catch fish there were in no wise different from those used to catch them from some still waters anyway, and although tench thrive in many rivers, there does not seem to be any specially devised method more suited to their capture.

I have caught, or seen caught, tench from the Rivers Ouse, Thame, Thames, Stour and Kennet. I have heard and read reports of their capture from many other rivers and I have even observed them in the River Test. The Shannon in Ireland is noted for its tench and there are a number of Norfolk rivers which produce them regularly. I personally do not know of a river where I could go and deliberately fish for tench with anything like as much hope of success as I could from a hundred-and-one still waters, but this does not mean that river tench fishing is not worth pursuing.

As far as this book is concerned, however, it means that I must discuss river tench fishing in general terms instead of selecting one particular water and describing my experiences there, as I have done in other chapters. To do so would only serve to bore the reader with repetitive accounts of the capture of very moderate fish. From the catches I have made and seen made, accidental or otherwise, however, it seems to me that there is very little to be gained from seeking tench in any but the slackest or slowest moving sectors of any river. This does not always apply in winter, however, as I will explain later.

I am quite convinced that the majority of tench are to be found in the wide slow-moving stretches of main rivers, in bays and slacks which the main current passes by and has little effect upon, in backwaters and cuttings separated from the main flow, and in holes in lilies and rush beds where the current is slowed down by the dense weed growth. These are typical tench haunts. There will be others, of course, and although I have never seen tench in such places, I am quite sure that they are likely to be present in the deep and quiet water immediately above some weir pools.

In my early days fishing the Thame it was not unusual to catch a small tench when laying-on with worms for roach or perch in the early hours of a summer's morning. Nor was it unheard of to catch one on a fixed line set for eels in the same river, but it was not tench fishing and no credit could be given for the capture of such fish. Fishing in those days, however, followed a fairly strict pattern. We would walk the river travelling light. Our baits would be brandlings, bread-paste, lobworms and occasionally (if we buried a few rabbit skins or paunches) some particularly vile-smelling maggots.

We never sat down to fish – nor did we use groundbait. We simply kept well back from the water's edge and dropped our floats into the many holes in the big lily beds and let them trot round the big wide corners. Almost invariably we caught roach. Sometimes it was perch. Once in a while we would catch a bream and, very rarely, a tench. The tactics used were the same always; only the bait was ever changed and I cannot think of anything else we might have done to increase our chances with the tench and lessen them with other fish. Not that we ever wanted to. We went fishing in those early days to catch fish. Specialization came later.

Before the upper Great Ouse was dredged and to all intents and purposes ruined as a fishery in the 1960s it was a great joy for my friends and me to fish the big holes in the bulrush beds for anything that came along. The roach were of good quality. We did not expect two pounders but pounders were common. We fished for them with big knobs of yellow paste, custard powder worked into plain bread paste, and the fish had a liking for it at evening time. Every so often would come a bite, no different from the rest, and the result would be a tench around the three pounds mark. In the confined spaces of the rush pockets, these tench fought like veritable tigers on roach tackle. It was a pleasure to catch them, but again, they were bonus fish.

The Waterfall, the cutting off the River Thame referred to in an earlier chapter, was different inasmuch as the tench could be caught intentionally. So too could the tench in a backwater of the Thames above Oxford. Here the river had taken a wide bend in years gone by and this had been cut through either by dredging or erosion so that a wide horseshoe bend was left which the main current missed. It was almost, but not quite, still water. It filled quickly with rushes, reeds, lilies and softweed and after a time became full of tench and rudd which apparently found their way in from the main river. Here it was possible to fish for, and catch, tench by design. They responded to lift tactics and baits of crust, maggots and worms. We fished for them, in fact, just as we would have fished for tench in any number of small ponds we knew.

Once, when fishing the middle Ouse at Offord in winter, I hooked and lost a moderate tench and heard of another angler upstream who had hooked and landed three that day.

I had always fancied that there might be some fair tench fishing there in summer, but had never managed to fish because of other commitments. I learned, afterwards, that numbers of tench are taken from there each year, again largely by accident, by freelance and match anglers alike, and I was further assured by a letter from angler Alan Jenkinson who wrote to me at some length on the subject.

The following is an extract from a letter he wrote to me some years ago:

My favourite venue is the middle Ouse near Offord, where the river runs deep, wide and very slow. There is little midwater weed, but the edges are thick with rushes, and lily beds are quite extensive.

During the two previous seasons, I noticed other anglers caught the occasional tench, mainly on their second rod which was usually fished near the bank for anything which came along, while their main efforts were devoted to catching bream from mid-stream.

As the quality of roach and bream from this stretch is not high, I decided to concentrate on tench, to see how prolific they were, and commenced at dawn on June 16th. I used a 12 ft rod, and legered with a size 8 hook tied direct to 5 lb b.s. line, and an Arlesey bomb, $\frac{1}{8}$ oz. stopped 30″ from the hook. Bait was lobworm.

Before fishing I baited a line about seven yards directly in front of my swim which was on an outside bend of the river. Then I cast the tackle slightly downstream of the groundbait, and near the edge of the lily pads, bordering the swim. The bite indicator was silver paper on a long loop of line between reel and butt ring.

The first bite was not long in coming, and was very strong and fast without any preliminary nibbling. It was a tench of $2\frac{3}{4}$ pounds.

I caught one more tench that morning, within half an hour of the first.

Tactics throughout the season were more or less as above, with the occasional use of bread bait as an alternative. Various common factors became apparent during subsequent visits, however, and tench became almost predictable. Firstly it was noticeable that they fed mainly in the early morning. The only exception to this was a dull rainy day in August when tench were coming to the net regularly until we packed up at 5 p.m. I never caught any tench during the evenings. In fact this venue is generally unproductive in the evening for any species. However the intensity of light seems to be an important factor. Next was that all bites were bold and fast, with no preliminaries at all, and striking them was comparatively easy.

Maybe the nature of the bottom of the river is unusual. That is the only way in which I can account for tench giving no clue at all to their presence. Not only did they *not* bubble at all, but did not even appear to move among the lily beds. If they did, they did so very carefully. Perhaps the fact that the stems are at least 6 ft long would account for it. Anyway, the first bite indication was a firm pull which was hard to miss.

All in all it was, for me, a successful season with only one blank day at this venue. Although the average weight was about $2\frac{1}{2}$ lbs they were all nice, clean, hard fighting fish, and I only failed to catch tench on two visits; I am convinced that this was because I arrived late on both occasions.

Incidentally, by concentrating on margin fishing, I added another bonus by occasionally catching bream which were above the average size for the water, on tackle meant for tench. Although not large bream, they certainly helped to increase my pleasure during a very enjoyable season.

Tench have been caught in all types of weather on this stretch during the winter and summer by other anglers, and weather permitting I shall continue fishing for them this coming season until it ends in March.

His thinking was obviously sound; his strategy correct. There is nothing new about his method of fishing, but here is proof that in at least one sector of one river, tench can be taken regularly by design as well as accident. I suspect there are many other rivers where the same interest and the same approach would produce similar results. What does it matter that the tench only averaged two and a half pounds? This is probably a fair average weight for the water, and anyway the object was to catch tench, not records.

Some young friends of mine once set siege on the barbel of the River Stour in Hampshire. They had it all planned and were very confident that, with permission to fish through the night, they would succeed. At that time very few barbel were being caught.

They baited a swim rather heavily with worms and bread before fishing, and during the dark hours they legered with lobworm hookbaits. But they had forgotten about the eels! Worm baits at night did not prove to be very good barbel baits but they certainly attracted eels!

The natural thing to do was change hookbaits and this they did. Cheese, a good barbel bait, still attracted eels, however, and only when they changed to ordinary bread baits did they stop catching them. They then caught tench instead!

I will not say that tench were unheard of there, but they were rarely reported in catches on that particular fishery. I have no idea how many tench were caught that week, but it was a considerable number. Every night saw at least one caught and by the middle of the week the group were discussing the next night's *tench* fishing! I watched the water closely one day myself. I was in the district on an entirely different venture, but called to see how things were progressing. I looked from high above into the clear water and saw two tench swimming idly around one of the hookbaits. They were not interested.

I suppose there was a reason for these tench not feeding by day but I cannot name it. They seemed to be truly nocturnal feeders and I suspect that this is true of tench in other really clear waters.

Some of the deep slower reaches of the Kennet have yielded tench at night but rarely during the day. The tench I saw in the Test one day were not in the least interested in food, but obviously they would have to feed sometimes and it is my opinion that they did so at night.

So some sort of sketchy pattern seems to begin to form and I believe it is worth looking into the common factors involved. Tench obviously do live in rivers and in the right conditions they can obviously be caught. Every year they are caught following winter floods from rivers which do not normally yield them in summer. The water is then quite coloured, but this is probably not the reason. More likely it is because they have been disturbed by the extra water, and I shall have more to say about this in Chapter 16. Meanwhile the river tench which I have caught and seen caught have these things in common. They have come from slowly moving or virtually still sectors as might be expected; and they have been taken either in darkness, or from waters which are naturally on the murky side during the day.

If I had to set out to prove a point and catch some river tench, these are the factors I would look for; but as I have always had access to still waters holding larger numbers of better quality tench, I do not see much point in it.

# 16 Winter Tench

A great many tench and carp are caught each season by anglers fishing for something entirely different, but more and more are being caught intentionally by those who are not entirely convinced that these are necessarily fish which feed only in summer. It is rather strange too that some of these winter caught carp and tench come from waters that do not normally produce them in summer.

I still regard winter carp fishing as something other people do, and I do not reckon to use up good time, which can be better spent in search of other species, trying to catch fish which are hard enough to catch in summer anyway. But this does not mean that I have not the greatest admiration for those who do practise it.

On the other hand, I have given a lot of thought to winter tench fishing during the past twenty years or so and, though I cannot claim to have achieved anything spectacular in this field, I think I have learned a little. There are a few common factors that appear to apply to all the winter tench I've caught, or with which I have been associated.

It occurs to me that, somehow or other, winter tench have to be *disturbed* before they will feed.

Consider the question of the river tench which turn up each winter. Almost without exception they come either during, or immediately after, a flood, and it would appear to be fairly obvious that the extra water coming down has moved them out of retirement. They have then had to fight the current for a while before settling again, and once active, quite naturally, they have fed. That is how it appears to me and to many other anglers who have encountered this situation.

Now consider the tench of still waters. They are not really likely to be disturbed by floods or other natural happenings, but it is possible to liven them up in other ways.

I remember, some years ago, a fellow angler having a fair amount of success with winter tench in a big still water. He said that he 'woke them up' with a rake or drag before fishing. He suffered some ridicule from unbelievers, but he caught enough tench to convince me that it was practical, at least, in some waters.

There is one particular water where I can be almost certain to catch tench all through the winter providing I go the right way about it. It is a local pit just about a mile from my home and my best winter tench session came one November. On that day I went to catch a few pike baits but stayed on longer and ended up by catching four tench. Pike baits are usually very easy to catch here. They are mostly rudd, but there are some roach as well which, though hungry, are not at all stupid. I can catch them on substantial tackle sometimes, but I have to wait a long time between fish and even then, all too often, the bites come from very small fish which somehow do not quite manage to pull the float under properly. This results in plenty of missed bites and a certain amount of frustration. I have found that it pays me right from the start to get busy with small hooks and fine tackle, especially if I want to stay on and catch tench eventually.

I use a no. 18 hook to a link of about $1\frac{1}{2}$ lb breaking-strain, but I have at times scaled down to a no. 20 or no. 22! I have never gone smaller than that; my specimen hunting friends don't let me forget it as it is, but I have my reasons and I believe that, in these circumstances, I can have a lot more lively fishing and a greater chance of tench than if I stick with the heavier gear.

The pit is very little different from many other waters. It does not hold any *really* big fish, but it does hold some fair carp and quite a lot of tench, which naturally interest me. I have never caught a carp there after October but I have caught plenty of tench all through the season. I seldom get more than two at a sitting in winter but I find this reward enough because of the interesting way in which the fishing develops.

It follows a pattern most days inasmuch as the very small rudd are invariably the first to start feeding. When I say very small, I mean fish not much more than an inch long and I have to winkle those out as fast as I can, otherwise they drive me crazy! It is of little use putting them back; they just clamour to get caught again, so I put all I catch into the keepnet and gradually the average size increases until, eventually, I begin to catch some fair fish. After that the rudd are usually replaced by roach and, as time goes by, the quality gets a little better.

Meanwhile I keep feeding the swim with light cloud and maggots and the fish seldom let the single maggot hookbait reach the bottom. That is one of the effects of fishing with really fine tackle. The hookbait sinks naturally and behaves very little differently from the unattached maggots.

I *know* it is going to happen, of course, but I never know when! I am waiting for it, but it always takes me by surprise. A bite, no different from all the rest, tweaks the float and I strike, and that is where the similarity ends! This is no bait but a tench!

I have caught many hundreds of tench in my lifetime, and some of them have been fairly big. Some have been caught in situations which have made me tremble, but I do not believe any tench I have ever caught can match these little ones in the pits. They tear around like all get out, and there is no stoppng them on the tackle I use. I just have to bide my time and be very careful. It is not often they weigh much more than two pounds; although I have had them up to nearly three pounds by employing these tactics.

One would think, perhaps, that with tench willing to feed in winter, simple tench tactics would take them, but it is not so. They have to be *stimulated* into taking and they have to be encouraged to take at mid-water. Continual activity in the swim, in the form of groundbait, maggots and very lively small fish provides this stimulation. Tench are inquisitive, and in waters where they have a job to make ends meet because of the intense competition for food, they will move towards a disturbance, even in winter, in much the same way as a carp investigates the commotion around a piece of crust in summer.

The carp in the pit, very occasionally, do the same thing. I have hooked a few in dead of winter when engaged in a baiting session, but I have never managed to hold them on such delicate tackle. Usually the hook hold has given but I have been broken too.

Nowadays, with such great interest being shown in winter carp, I often wonder if such tactics might succeed in recognized carp waters, but for the time being I have enough problems with the tench! The more I think about it, however, the more I wonder if there are not many other waters where the tench might feed in winter if they were encouraged to do so.

A young Peter Drennan and a winter tench

I am quite sure that it is just a question of rousing them and that feeding an area regularly, and disturbing the water by catching lots of small fish, is an effective way of doing so. Flood water coming down a river provides a natural means of disturbing tench from their winter state of semi-hibernation. A brisk 'tiddler snatching' session does the same thing in a different way on still waters.

All of which reminds me of a lake in Berkshire where Ken, Peter Stone, Peter Drennan and I used to catch tench regularly in winter, by design and quite irrespective of conditions. We never failed except when the water was completely frozen.

The lake was fed through a sluice gate from the Kennet and Avon canal. It overflowed into the River Kennet at the opposite end, and we were able to control the flow by opening or closing the sluice gates.

We discovered the tench largely by accident when we were pike fishing one cold January day. We wondered if opening the sluice might liven up the pike and so we opened it to full bore. The level rose rapidly, the water turned muddy, and we realized at once that we'd probably spoiled our chances of pike that day. Quite suddenly, however, tench began to roll on the surface and we figured there and then that if tench would roll in January, they would feed too. We were right.

We caught them that day on maggots and fine tackle which we fished hard on the bottom despite their surface rolling. From then on we caught them whenever we wished in winter, even when the banks were white and hard with frost. We never had large numbers, but they were all good fish and very strong fighters. The most we ever caught in a day was five averaging over three and a half pounds.

Here again the 'basic formula' of disturbing the tench seemed to apply. We knew that once we could start them rolling on the surface, we could catch them, and it was a peculiarity of that water that the tench invariably surfaced sooner or later once the sluice was open.

Of recent years, I have been thinking that perhaps the summer species of a good many other waters could be 'brainwashed' into feeding in winter by a little disturbance now and then. Would carp respond to raking tactics for instance, or would the disturbance scare the daylights out of them like it does in summer? I often wonder, too, what would be the result of opening up the sluices of some other tench lakes I know.

There are, of course, many waters where the tench populations are heavy and the fish undernourished. These are usually modest ponds where there is no predation and where the tench appear able to reproduce in large numbers unhindered. These waters almost invariably produce tench all year round. For some reason, probably the sheer need for survival, the fish do not seem to slow down or 'hibernate' in winter; and generally speaking little skill is required to catch them. They are small and hungry; some of them appear to have reached a reasonable size and then 'gone back'. They have been unable to maintain their body weight and eventually have become large headed, thin-bodied, and pathetically out of condition. In the main, however, the tench in these waters manage to reach a certain standard of fitness and though small, they are nicely shaped and appear to be in reasonable condition. They do not interest me because they have no sporting value. I often refer to them as 'tiddlers' but I should make it quite clear that they are *not* immature tench. They are adult fish that, despite year round feeding, will never grow big.

Those are the only 'tiddler' tench we are likely to see in natural conditions for, as I have already observed, 'tiddler tench' appear to be non-existent in waters which produce numbers of quality specimens year after year.

What puzzles me, however, is the occasional really big tench that turns up in one of these modest ponds. There's no apparent reason why one tench should grow twice, or even three times as big as the rest, but just once in a while it happens that way.

I suppose we could dismiss it by referring to small men and giants. Occasionally a man grows to seven feet without any apparent reason (certainly not because he eats more food) and we accept the fact that he's just a big fellow. But it is, I believe, different with fish.

In every situation I know where fish are fed artificially, there are always a few that are quicker off the mark or able in some way to get more food than the rest. These are the fish that grow big. In other words their growth rate is in keeping with their food intake. Tench, feeding naturally in a small pond, would have no such opportunity and it is doubtful if one fish, or one group of fish, could over-exploit the food supply.

It might just be possible, however, that these big fish have learned to exploit an entirely *different* food source, and I am reminded here of an estimated seven pounder (mentioned in Chapter 14) which undoubtedly took a portion of dead rudd. *That* tench had a liking for something entirely different from what is generally regarded as normal tench diet – which *might* have been the reason for its unusual proportions. I don't think chunks of fish will ever replace worms and paste as baits for tench but the idea is perhaps worthy of consideration.

# 17 Future Developments?

So what of the future of tench fishing? Throughout this book I have briefly mentioned small changes in the tackles employed on different waters and of the gradual development of tench-fishing equipment over the years.

Silk lines have been replaced by monofilament, and today's strong nylon allows for fishing a great deal finer than that which we first practised with our soaked-gut casts and greased silk. They will get even better as time goes by . . . .

I started fishing with half a roach pole, graduated to a heavy greenheart, progressed to tonkin and built-cane via home-made steel tank-aerial rods; toyed with straight-taper hollow glass and have settled, for the time being, on the superb compound-tapered hollow glass rods being produced by Hardy's and others at the time of writing. I say 'for the time being' because interesting developments are going ahead with carbon fibre and glass fibre composites. Rod developments in this material are still progressing but ultra-lightweight, long versions are already available and proving popular in situations where the rod has to be held continually and not set in rests.

Tench floats have seen change since I first began fishing. The ones we used then have disappeared. Bird and porcupine quills are still with us, so are the lengths of peacock quill known as lift floats. May supplies never run out!

More consistent and reliable floats are now being manufactured in balsawood, however, and specialists' requirements are being met by knowledgeable manufacturers like P. J. Drennan of Oxford. With them have come new techniques.

Landing-net frames have progressed from small crude wire rings to the modern Apex design by Efgeeco of South London. These may be bought with arms as long as thirty-two inches; large enough for any tench that swims, and particularly useful at night.

John Mason puts a Wotton tench into a modern knotless keepnet

Keepnets, too, have improved beyond recognition. Gone are those tiny rusty ringed net cages which were crammed to capacity when more than one fair sized tench was introduced. They have been replaced by capacious nets, six, eight and sometimes ten feet long, and wide in proportion. Their rings are of plastic or plastic covered wire and they are more than adequate for most situations. Soft knotless nylon has replaced cotton and today's keepnets are highly

Big catches of tench are better released quickly but this home-made early keepnet did our fish no harm

unlikely to cause harm to fish. Only when the weave is too fine and becomes clogged can damage occur.

I am reminded here of a big keepnet I once made from a 280 lb wheat sack and a bicycle wheel. It often accommodated as many as forty tench and not one of them ever suffered harm in its dark soft interior!

Hooks are probably much the same as they were twenty or more years ago, although more eyed and spade hooks are being tied directly to reel lines for bigger fish these days. Rightly so, of course. Casts, hook-links and other joins between the hook and the reel line proper, simply serve to weaken the line. By tying hooks direct, a finer line can be used with less chance of breakage.

It is doubtful if I shall ever find the hook I really seek, but by and large those I use for tench are fairly reliable. I have pinned my faith for many years now on some fine-wire blue spades by Mustad. I can tie them in complete darkness because I do not have to thread my line through any eye, and I have found them to be fairly consistent from batch to batch. But I am always on the lookout for something better.

So much for tackle then; but what of future fishing developments?

I see the need for a special lamp for illuminated float fishing at night and Dick Walker is convinced that some form of diffused beam could be perfected which would render the light almost invisible to anyone other than the operator. I can only wait and hope that he goes to work and produces one!

I have put one minor, but very interesting tackle development to the test in recent years. It is a virtually snag-free float tackle devised by Ken Taylor for perch and rudd fishing. The line is threaded completely through a piece of peacock quill with a big baiting needle and this is stopped from sliding down by a big swan shot pinched on immediately below it. This completes a self-cocking rig which can be drawn between reed and rush stems without becoming caught up, and which can be cast very accurately with an underhand swing. It is a most useful rig for fishing slow-sinking baits in the margins when the sun is high; and I am now able to fish difficult spots with a lot more confidence.

And what of method itself? New float methods must be the subject of a complete chapter, but what others are likely to develop in the near future? American methods are being practised more and more for the predatory fish of this country and there is much talk of seeking our carp with lures and jigs such as the Americans use. But will tench fishing ever undergo any real change? The habitat and behaviour of the tench seem to suggest not, but let us consider the situation.

Tench fishing, to me, has always incurred a great deal in the way of preparation. Good tench waters are weedy, shallow, and consequently very fertile. Their beds are usually (but not always) of thick mud and this undoubtedly seems to encourage soft weed growth which, in turn, encourages tench to laze, graze, and grow fat. To reach tench in these waters it is necessary to clean and bait a swim, preferably several days before fishing. Indeed, by doing things properly, well in advance, it is possible to guarantee that tench will be present when the time comes to fish. So there seems to be no point in trying to make things even more difficult by fishing with lures and the like.

It will always be necessary to work on tench swims of this nature; without weed-clearance, lures and jigs could never reach the bottom, but I wonder sometimes if life could not be made a little more interesting by employing different tactics *after* the clearing has been done.

I do not suppose I shall ever stop using the extensive pre-baiting methods I have always used over the past twenty years or so, when I have really been out for blood. I do not expect I shall ever stop carrying big loads of groundbait either, but I am thinking now in terms of a lighthearted approach to tench fishing.

I have made it quite clear throughout this book that I regard tench as inquisitive creatures, and that there are many situations where they can be encouraged into a swim simply by stirring up the bottom. This means that, given reasonable conditions, tench begin to poke around in a swim shortly after it has been cleared of weed, and if things go right, they can often be caught in the midst of their enthusiastic foragings.

A particular incident comes to my mind. It happened late one season in 1967 and the situation was one wherein my brother Ken and I had had very little time to spare for swim preparation. We were without groundbait because of a snap decision. We had been fishing for summer pike using surface lures, and tench were farthest from our minds at that time. It was a very hot day, the lake was unoccupied and we decided to swim for a while, in an area of shallow water about twenty yards out from the bank. A little weed was visible, but, probably because of the tree-lined bank, it was not very thick. The boat had drifted there of its own accord and the choice of spot was not really of our own making. A prod or two with the oar, however, indicated a soft mud bottom and at this stage both Ken and I began to wonder about tench.

The only baits we had with us were a few maggots which had been used to catch some small pike baits earlier. Not much for a tench fishing session, but we felt compelled by the circumstances to give it a whirl. It seemed, perhaps, that fate had decreed it.

We swam for perhaps half an hour and generally stirred up the mud bottom. Any weed in that small area was soon ripped out and pretty soon the water was churned to a black muddy goo. We let it settle while we swam to the boathouse to clean up, towing the boat behind us.

Later, we approached the swim quietly and anchored a few rod lengths out. The water had cleared a little, but there were patches of bubbles coming to the surface in several places. The tench had arrived!

To cut a long story short we caught those tench, about a dozen of them, on fine tackle and the few maggots we had left. We did *not* use groundbait and this made it one of the most interesting tench-fishing sessions I have ever experienced.

I was once accused of never mentioning the word maggots in connection with tench fishing; a lot of nonsense, of course, because I have used and mentioned them many times. When I have used them, however, I have always felt that I should use a lot and spread them out generously as free offerings all over the swim. Good tactics these, and ones that usually pay off, but on this day we could not really afford to throw any into the water.

We caught those tench on baits fished on the bottom, on baits that sank slowly through the still murky water, and on baits that were retrieved slowly along the bottom. Undoubtedly the stationary bottom-fished baits accounted for the most fish. That way the tench could inspect the maggots, decide that they were real and fit to eat, and finally accept them. But, I wonder, could they have made the same inspection of the slowly sinking baits or those that were being retrieved along the bottom?

In this book I have described several occasions when tench preferred a moving bait. It may have been sinking on a leadless tackle, or drifting with the breeze under a float. It may have been a twitched or slowly retrieved bait, but the truth is that it didn't matter too much what kind of bait it was as long as it moved. In these circumstances does a tench *know* what it is taking? Does it have time to inspect the bait before it takes? Does it take the moving bait because it is already suspicious of the still one? I do not know the answers to these questions, but they tempt me to think again about other forms of fishing for tench.

I have had ideas about fly fishing for coarse fish other than the accepted fly-takers for a long time, and soon I hope to try it for tench. I am quite sure that it will never take the place of traditional

A drifting bait on light tackle accounted for this tench

float or leger fishing, nor will it ever be as effective, but it ought to be fun. Will tench take flies? The answer could probably be a Joadian 'It all depends on what you mean by flies'.

Tench have been known to take surface flies, but dry-fly fishing could hardly be considered a tench-fishing method. On the other hand, nymphs and tiny pupæ imitations, fished deeply, might well account for tench which were foraging over a muddy bottom.

I remember Dick Walker catching some tiny tench on small green nymphs at Two Lakes. Others have had the same experience, I believe, and there is no reason to believe that big tench, if they had been present, would not have taken the same offerings. These nymphs were tied to imitate natural creatures found in the water, but is it necessary, I wonder, to be so particular? Maggots are not normally found in lakes, and I am absolutely certain that none had ever been introduced to the tench swim I have just described, but the tench took those we used on our hooks immediately. So, without being too fussy, what would be wrong with tying a fly to look like a maggot? It could be white, pink, yellow or green and it could even be fished in conjunction with a handful of natural maggots anyway. I see no wrong in this and my brother Ken has already tied me some! I think the pleasure to be derived from catching a big tench on a trout fly rod would justify a little 'cheating' in the form of a handful or two of 'encouragement'.

I can remember, years ago taking roach from the Ouse on an artificial maggot. It was a wool and rubber concoction which really did look like a maggot. It only worked 'on the trot' and then only when the swim was fed liberally with natural maggots. All of which makes me think that a nicely tied imitation maggot, fished on a sinking line through a recognized tench swim, would be in with more than a chance of success.

From the lake in question I have taken rudd on flies, both on the surface and sunk. They, too, like the little green nymphs Dick Walker ties and I have had some success with a particular red-tagged grayling fly tied by Ken. Sometimes I have caught the rudd by approaching the margins cautiously in the boat and casting to them. Other times I have 'cheated' and scattered a few crusts around to get the rudd interested. Watching them attack those crust portions, and remembering the numbers of tench I have caught on floating crust, I have often wondered if some ingenious fly-dresser could not fashion a fly to imitate a piece of bread! After all it *has* been known for trout anglers to tie flies that look like pieces of horsemeat in order to tempt newly introduced stew fish!

I remember too, a long time ago, a Mr Webb sending me some imitation casters or chrysalids. They were fashioned from balsawood, slit and attached to an appropriate eyed hook. They were tied with a spiral of gossamer silk to imitate the rings on the body of a natural caster. They were stained bright red and then covered with shellac varnish which gave them a final colouring of natural perfection. My wife, seeing them nestling on their bed of foam, once started to throw out 'those disgusting maggot things' but I rescued them in time!

I used these in conjunction with natural floating chrysalids, and if Mr Webb reads this, I would like him to know that I had a lot of fun with them but never managed to make any quite as good.

But do you see what's going through my mind? Tench will take natural sinking casters; why not an artificial tied to look like one?

With these thoughts buzzing around my head (and they do not upset me like they might upset someone with purist tendencies) I believe that I can hope for a lot of fun in fly fishing for tench. I reserve the right to clear a swim before I start to fish and if (and only if) I think my chances might be improved by so doing I may introduce some natural maggots or chrysalids as well and then fish with a dressed artificial.

How will I dress them? Frankly I don't know and in any case I shan't have to worry, because I have Dick and my brother Ken to help out in this respect. But I have some idea as to what the things should look like, having examined a lot of 'nymphy' creatures from various tench waters. Dick Walker has often said we do not try hard enough with fly tackle for coarse fish and I believe he is right when he says that *all* fish could be pursued in this fashion, sometimes with even better results than we would at first anticipate.

Well, I'm going to have a try. I'm not a very good fly fisherman but I enjoy trying (sometimes my friends say I'm *very* trying), and I intend, if I am spared, to see what can be done about it. And I'll stick my neck out here and now and say that, if I have a fair opportunity, I will eventually catch tench on flies.

I'm as confident as that, but meanwhile two important issues need discussing before this book is ended. Baits and float techniques have all been mentioned in passing. Now let us look at them more closely and with modern tench fishing in mind.

# 18 Baits and Groundbaits

You can, in favourable circumstances and with a little bit of craft, spot a tench in the water and, with no more than a bait on a leadless tackle, catch it. You may do the same with chub, trout or carp with a much greater chance of success. The fish you can see are often the fish you can catch because they're feeding fish. Not always, but often. Fishing is then more of a hunt and you spend your time going after individual fish – one from here and one from there. It's different from the kind of tench fishing most of us practise today – seated in a chosen swim and waiting for the fish to come to us. Fishing probably started as a hunting exercise and there are still many kinds of fish that respond to the hunter's approach, but to compile real bags of coarse fish we have developed the business of groundbaiting to a pretty fine degree.

There are, and always will be, areas of water that hold very few if any fish for most of the year, and yet today's special groundbaits, allied to patience and good hookbait presentation, will take fish from these spots. You wouldn't catch fish from them without groundbait, because you cannot catch fish from them without groundbait, because you cannot catch a fish that isn't there! Groundbait, therefore, is a substance used to attract fish from somewhere else. True or false?

It's true, of course, but it's a big mistake to think that this is its only function. Groundbait can also be used to good effect on fish that are already in the swim. It doesn't *attract* them; it starts them feeding.

Two jobs, important jobs, both concerned with putting fish in the net, but very different application.

There are dozens, maybe hundreds, of different situations demanding special groundbaiting techniques and it would be impossible to dwell on them all here, but we can perhaps look at a couple of extreme situations while bearing in mind that groundbait is a term used loosely to cover a whole field of fishing with 'free offerings'.

It includes such things as maggots, casters, breadcrumbs, multi-meal mixes, chopped worms, sweetcorn, beans, wheat, cheese portions, lumps of pinched bread, loose bread crusts and so forth. Sweetcorn, maggots and casters are among today's most popular baits. Brandlings and lobworms are also high up on the list and the probable reason for their popularity is that they are easily acquired. You just go into the tackle shop and buy them. The maggots and casters sold today are generally top quality, consistent baits that serve both as hookbait and free offering. Groundbaits come in many forms and represent good value for money even at today's prices. It should be remembered, however, that different mixes have different roles to play and that choice of groundbait must depend upon the nature of the fishing.

Some mixes are designed to attract but not to feed. Others are designed to act as feed and to hold feeding fish in a given area.

There are waters where you simply cannot carry enough bait to hold a shoal of tench, and others where a pound of lightly mixed cloud bait will last all day. Circumstances and situations differ considerably and using the right groundbaiting technique is of great importance.

If, for instance, you have cleared a great hole in the weedbeds in the hopes of catching tench, you have to introduce enough good, solid groundbait to draw the fish into the open water and start them feeding on something substantial. There are exceptions, of course, but despite what has been written about other situations, tench *are* mainly bottom feeders and if you want to get them working in the swim you need a good tight groundbait that breaks up slowly on the bottom. You can include maggots or casters, sweetcorn or worms in the mix if you like and there's no reason why you should not stretch a proprietary brand of groundbait considerably by using it simply as a drying agent for soaked and squeezed bread. Basically the object here is to draw the fish and get them feeding in the swim. The hookbait itself does not *have* to be the same as the groundbait – though there is one proprietary multi-mix groundbait that makes up into an excellent paste.

This paste makes a very satisfactory hookbait when used in conjunction with the groundbait itself. But lobworms, breadcrust, maggots, or almost any other kind of hookbait will serve in this

Weed clearing with a portable drag

situation. Some experiment will be necessary, of course, as there will undoubtedly be days when the fish show a preference, but the object is to present the hookbait as the 'plum' piece – more attractive than the groundbait carpet which drew the fish in the first place. A point worth considering here is the colour of the groundbait. Many anglers want a pure white carpet that the fish can see from a long way off. My own feelings are that many fish are reluctant to swim over such areas because they beome prone to attacks from pike! A darker mix in these circumstances may be better in the long run.

An entirely different situation arises when you're faced with – say – a shoal of tench cruising at mid-water and not strictly foraging. Occasionally they, or one of them, will snap at a passing item of food and it is here that the technique known as loose feeding is more practicable.

Introducing a few items of food, sweetcorn, maggots, casters (whatever you have available), and doing it in a manner that does not arouse suspicion is the most likely road to success. There are times when it will all be in vain, but as long as the shoal remains or cruises the area returning at intervals, it is a tactic well worth trying.

To encase the free offerings (which should be identical seed or particle baits), in a great wodge of groundbait to reach distant fish will disperse the shoal nine times out of ten. If the shoal is well out, use a maggot catapult, and *don't* overdo the dosage. Get the fish interested, watch to see if they intercept the sinking particles, and then gradually decrease the distance to try and draw them closer to the bank.

It may be found that gradually, as the feed settles on the bottom, the tench will drop down and begin to pick up rather than intercept sinking portions. But there are no hard and fast rules.

Loose feeding is a tiring but highly skilled exercise. Not everyone has the temperament for it. Those who have mastered it, and allied it to modern float techniques, have changed the whole tench fishing scene on some waters. Whether that is for the good or not I hesitate to say. If it is the only *means* of taking fish, obviously it is for the good; but littering vast areas with gallons of maggots and causing big fish like tench to become temporarily preoccupied with single maggots which, in order to be presented properly, can only be fished on fine tackle and tiny hooks, does little to improve general tench fishing. In heavily weeded and snaggy waters, it results in many lost fish which might otherwise have been caught on substantial baits and tackle.

Which is why I pin my faith very much at the beginning of the season on lobworms. I use other baits, of course, but to me there is no substitute for a lob during the early season. I have success with lobs because I know how to keep them in good condition and I know that every lobworm I present to a tench is one of top quality.

I do not believe they are in any way superior to other baits, but the facts are that they can be presented on substantial tackle, tench like them, and in a traditional early-season, baited swim they are readily accepted baits. I have already told of situations where other baits and other presentations will produce more tench than the bottom fished lobworm, and I am not suggesting here that the lobworm must always be fished on the bottom. If you have read thus far into this book you will know that it is not so. You will also know that there are waters where lobworms are *not* so readily accepted. But when I see some anglers at the waterside with what they proudly refer to as their 'supply of lobs' I almost weep for them! Collecting and keeping lobs is almost an art! *Do* take the trouble to learn it!

They are not always readily available. Most tackleists try to maintain supplies, but they are entirely dependent upon the collectors who in turn are dependent upon the weather.

If long, dry spells bake the ground hard there's little hope of a regular worm supply, which is all the more reason why you should look after those you happen to have. And if you collect your own

'Pulling' lobworms at night

from wet lawns or gardens after dark you should take care to make sure that each one is serviceable.

One hears talk of 'pulling' worms at night. It's an old expression and many worms *are* actually *pulled* from the ground each season. It doesn't take too much experience, however, to realize that you must *not* pull too hard. Otherwise you'll end up with half a worm instead of a whole one! You learn, as you tread lightly across paths and lawns, that vibrations send the worms back into their holes with incredible rapidity, and you need to move very quickly to nail a worm that's lying half in and half out of its hole. When you grab it, you're inclined to grab it hard and hold it tightly for fear it may escape, but that is almost as bad as *pulling* too hard. Pinched worms are damaged worms and although some may recover in time, they can go bad and ruin the whole supply. That's why it always grieves me to see anglers who are so particular about the way they buy, prepare and take care of their maggots and casters, neglect lobworms to such an extent that even their chances of survival are doubtful!

If you've spent good money on lobworms, bought from a reputable tackle shop, you can be fairly sure that you've got good quality worms, value for money, and that when they're handed over to you they're in good shape. The collector and the tackleist have gone to some trouble to see to that; but from then on it's all down to you. And if you take your hundred worms, cram them into a small bait tin, and then fish all day in the hot sun, you need not expect to have many fit for use next day! Worms do not take kindly to being overcrowded, they do not take kindly to being overheated and they do not take kindly to becoming dry.

They need room (there's a special exception to this rule which I'll discuss later), they need a temperature of around 45°F. (there is latitude either way, 55°F. is the absolute top limit regarding safety, and of course there should be no question of frosting) and they need a reasonable amount of moisture.

Accepted worm-keeping lore suggests the use of fresh moss and many of the old books insist that lobs should be well scoured for several days before use. Scouring lobs in moss will do little harm provided the right conditions are maintained, but all this business is quite unnecessary, and it doesn't improve the worms at all! Moss is a pleasant enough medium in which to keep a day's supply but I wouldn't recommend it for long-term storage. Moss *can* heat up by combustion – particularly if it gets mixed up with other organic material – and if it does you'll be left only with the smell! There's no reason, however, why you should not buy worms when they're freely available and store them for use later. Just remember that several hundred lobworms having 'gone wrong' can be a stinking and embarrassing mess!

If you are fortunate enough to be able to collect your own when conditions are right, you can, by careful storage, maintain supplies for a whole year or more. I have kept a supply of lobs for a full year just to prove it was possible, and while I won't try to convince anyone that they were in as good a shape as when they were first collected, they were still good, fishable worms. I have my own ideas about worm storage, and they're the result of a good many years' experience but I regard collection as the number one priority. Start off with sound worms and you'll keep a good supply; start off with pinched or stretched worms and you'll always have trouble. It's probably easier said than done, but if professional worm catchers can produce 100% good quality, undamaged worms, so can you. Talk to the professional and he'll tell you that he's sitting indoors watching television or having a snooze while the amateur is out snatching and pulling at worms still only half way out! The professional waits his time. He *picks up* his worms; he doesn't *pull* them. It may mean a later night – an hour or two less sleep – but if it results in a supply of good worms it's well worth the wait. Once worms are fully out, lying on the ground or grass, there's no need for speed and frantic grabbing. Those worms are there for the picking.

It doesn't always happen that way, of course. There are nights when worms don't come out at all (dry nights, windy nights, very cold nights) and there are nights when, despite what appear to be ideal conditions, they still refuse to come completely out. But every so often there comes the night of soft warm rain when every worm for miles around comes up to revel on the wet surface. Sports fields, grass verges, lawns, gardens, golf courses, even meadows where sheep have kept the grass short, then produce super worm yields. Those nights are worth waiting for, even if it does mean lack of sleep followed by severe backache! But *do* wait until it's right. Go out and check every half hour or so to see if the worms are *fully* out; if not give them a bit longer.

The situation may occasionally develop in the wrong direction, of course. You may find that instead of coming out further during the interval, they've been slowly withdrawing and that you've missed the peak period. But that's the way it goes. There's little you can do about it. Some subtle change has perhaps taken place that has gone unnoticed by you but which has adversely affected your 'harvest'.

At this point you may well consider that you should have made your move earlier and made the best of whatever opportunities were available at that time. And if the situation happens to be a desperate one in which you needed those worms badly – you may be right! Again, it's all down to you. In the long term I believe it pays to wait for the right time; to reap one good harvest without a great deal of struggle and frustration. And having collected a supply, it's essential to keep them in good shape and in a good compost.

I make my compost out of shredded newspaper and I find it keeps worms reasonably well for long periods. Many of the worm-keeping compounds used in the USA are based on powdered newspaper with 'foods' added, and there's no doubt about it, these composts are excellent, but torn-up newspaper *will* suffice, I assure you.

Would you believe there's a special way of tearing up a newspaper? If you pull it one way it comes away in chunks; if you pull it the other it comes away in long thin strips. This is the best way.

All you need do then is soak it thoroughly, squeeze it as dry as you can and put it into a big wooden or styrene box. You can put a whole newspaper on the bottom, add a layer of shreds, pop in, say, a hundred worms, lay on another whole newspaper and repeat the process to the capacity of your box. Worms need room and they'll be found at a later date tucked between the pages and curled up in corners. They'll usually head for the *bottom* of the box so it's a good idea if you have *two* lids. Then, because the newspaper is comparatively light, you can pick up the box, turn it upside down, open it at the bottom and cream off the day's supply. Then leave it that way up and the worms will make their way to the bottom again.

Keep the compost box out of the sun. In hot weather it will do nicely in a shady part of the garden or on a cold garage floor, but, if necessary, keep a couple of ice bottles for emergencies. Ordinary washing up liquid bottles, *three-quarters* filled with water and frozen in the ice compartment of the fridge make ideal cooler bottles. Alternate them *daily* during very hot weather. Stand the one in use upright in the compost and you'll find that the worms will, at times, home in on them, attracted to the cooler area. It sounds a bit of a bind, but it takes only a few seconds daily once you're organized.

And here's a tip about keeping and conditioning lobworms, which I believe will surprise you. I got the idea from the USA. Take a dozen worms, which may have dehydrated a bit in the compost, and pack them into a medium-sized bait-boxful of newspaper that has been saturated with *ice-cold* water (unchlorinated if possible). Centralize the worms and make sure the excess water is drained off (not squeezed out), then, making sure the soaked paper is just sufficient to make you *press* the lid of the box down to seal it, store the whole thing away in the refrigerator for two or three days. *Don't* let it freeze. If you can't use the refrigerator, take several of these boxes so packed and store them in an insulated box with ice bottles. *Always* make up more boxes than you're likely to need because, for some inexplicable reason, you get the odd box that goes wrong. After a few days of treatment (the Americans call it 'conditioning') the worms emerge fat and lively beyond all imagination. The whole secret lies in keeping them cold. They absorb moisture as they lie in their confined quarters and, while there's no 100% success guarantee, I believe it's well worth the gamble.

I've perhaps had too much to say about lobworms at the expense of other baits, but it is a fact that while many other baits can still be used even after being neglected, lobworms cannot. Maggots need keeping cool, but will turn to useful casters if they're forgotten. Paste, wheat and corn will go sour but still catch fish. Crust may go hard but can still be a useful hookbait. Brandlings don't suffer too much in the heat, but it does no harm to keep them in the shade. *Always* keep the lid on the box after dark, however, otherwise you'll find you've only the compost left.

I must, of course, refer briefly again to soaked and fermented maize. Indian maize is available in this country, and when soaked, left to ferment and smell, it becomes a very attractive form of loose feed. Tench eat it. It sometimes takes them a long time to accept it but they will stuff themselves so full of it that they almost rattle. I have suggested elsewhere in this book that soft sweetcorn should be used as hook bait in conjunction with soaked and fermented maize. I will further suggest that the sweetcorn hookbait should be allowed to soak with the maize so that it develops the same disgusting smell!

I could fill a book on tench baits alone, some natural, some traditional, some utterly stupid and of no value apart from their novelty. But I am sure of one thing. The tench angler who carries a variety of good baits and rings the changes regularly *will* catch fish on those days when tench are supposedly 'off'.

And, at the risk of boring the reader, I cannot end a chapter on baits without reference to the so-called, modern 'high protein baits'.

I do not believe, nor will I ever be convinced, that fish are capable of distinguishing between – say – protein and carbohydrate! The fact that certain baits with high protein content have been successful merely shows that they have proved attractive to fish and that, as such, they've been well worth using. I am not a dietician, but at one period during my life I was involved in dietry, and I know my way round diet sheets and calorie charts. I know the effects of fats, carbohydrates and protein on the body. I also know a little about animal foodstuffs having been associated with farming all my life, and I've come to the conclusion that many of the anglers who talk glibly of high protein baits do not even know what protein is! There are, of course, many who do, and I am not suggesting for one moment that there is total ignorance, but when I hear such baits as sweetcorn referred to as high protein I have to stop and think! Sweetcorn is possibly higher in protein than most other corn, but it is still substantially high-carbohydrate. Barley meal, I happen to know, contains only 6 per cent protein, and yet I have known anglers mix this with ordinary bread into a paste and refer to it as a high protein bait. It isn't!

If you mixed it with a percentage of fish meal (50 per cent protein) and Nigerian ground nuts (37 per cent protein) you could end up with a high protein paste. If you mixed it with a percentage of Urea synthetic protein you would have a bait with an even higher protein content. Urea protein is a short term feed commodity. It is comparatively cheap and my farming family and friends do not rate it highly for long term feeding, but that fact is quite irrelevant from the hookbait point of view.

Protein, so the dictionary says, is 'an organic compound forming the most essential part of food of animals', but of course fish and humans need it too. Soya beans are fairly high in protein, so too are ordinary field beans. Wheat and oats are low in protein, so it follows that pastes concocted from these meals will vary considerably and that although they can be adjusted and calculated, the ultimate protein content cannot be very high without additions.

Commercial high protein cattle food mixes *are* calculated and, of course, there are other necessary salts and vitamins added to them.

The breakdowns shown on the bags or containers give their exact protein content and, if anyone really considers it important enough, a study of these breakdowns might be worthwhile.

Trout pellets are high in protein. They contain a great deal of fish meal and, depending on the manufacturers, should comprise about 40 per cent protein. I wouldn't want to be too precise, but I'd think that's knocking the high limit of any commercial animal food product. If you could fish with a trout pellet on a hook you'd probably be fishing with a commercial bait as high in protein as is possible; but that's a very difficult exercise.

I'm aware of the old dodge involving hot needles and threading processes, and I know that it *is* possible to put the pellet on the hook; but unless you're expecting quick bites, it's not very practical. Trout pellets dissolve in water and a solid hookbait quickly becomes a little heap of mush. So, in order to fish pellets on the hook you have to make them into a paste with bread or meal or some binding ingredient which automatically lowers the protein percentage. As if it matters anyway!

The success of trout pellet groundbait and trout pellet paste hookbaits (and that's what many of these secret high protein baits are made of) lies in their attractive qualities – not in their protein content. If you cut off a slice of fish flesh, a chunk of boiled egg, a cube of cheese, or a piece of raw beef and stuck it on a hook, you'd be fishing with a high protein bait because it so happens that these are high protein foods.

It so happens, too, that I have caught fish on all these baits. One of the biggest tench I ever hooked (but unfortunately lost) was on a piece of freshly-killed rudd flesh. I've caught carp by the dozen in the USA on fish guts, chicken livers, fish roe and all other kinds of offal that just happens to be high in protein, but I do not believe that the carp considered the protein content!

A few special concoctions, dreamed up by extremely successful tench anglers, may be higher in protein than those I've mentioned here, and I'm not trying to make a case for or against their use. Confidence, in my opinion, is much more important than content. If you believe in a bait you'll catch more fish. And if you consider a high protein content important and have confidence in it, *of course* it will work better for you than a bait which doesn't have that quality.

It's so easy for a young angler, or a beginner, to become confused and 'blinded with science' regarding modern bait conceptions, but when you look back into angling history there's very little that hasn't been tried before. I place my faith in certain baits at certain times and in certain conditions, but I am quite sure in my own mind that field craft or water lore (call it what you like) is of more overall importance than bait content.

# 19 Float Developments

I have mentioned various floats in passing during the writing of this book. Some I have described fully, others I have left more or less to the reader's imagination; but while the subject of floats and float technique is an enormous one, considering *all* the types of fishable waters this country has to offer, many modern float developments cannot be applied to tench fishing.

Basically we need a float that will present a bait in still or very slow-moving water and register bites of different kinds. We do not have to compete with violent currents or turbulence. We do not have to consider how to trot through a swim under the far bank thirty yards distant, and we are hardly ever likely to require floats with a great deal of top buoyancy.

In a canal, where fishing under the rod tip pays good dividends, a simple crow quill shotted with a biggish shot pinched a few inches below it, and a much smaller one near to the hookbait, would be an ideal rig. The bait only need rest on the bottom and registration of a tench bite might be a slow lift or a quick dip. The big shot below the float acts as a 'depth setter' and helps cock the float quickly, while the smaller shot takes the bait down. In a situation where tench *are* feeding just off the bottom it works extremely well.

A small 'flat top', made of balsa and shotted down so that the merest dimple remains showing on the surface, is another good float for shy biting canal tench.

Regular lift method floats have already been described. They comprise a length of peacock quill attached at the bottom end only by a wide, tight-fitting band. They are set over-depth and all is drawn taut until they cock. A good lift float should sink slowly under the weight of the single cocking shot and the bait. Thus, the shot will always be resting on the bottom provided the float shows. The bite registers, as a lift, and an immediate strike is essential.

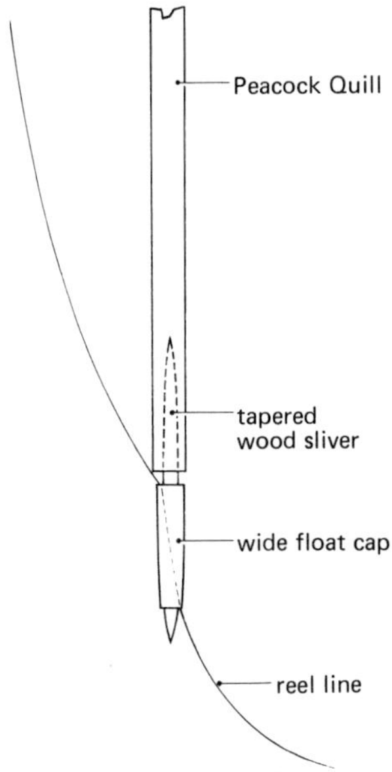


*Figure 8* Tapered hardwood insert for peacock quills

A problem invariably occurs when attaching the tight float cap to the peacock quill. The fibres are often crushed and the float ruined. An alternative, sent to me by a reader of *Angler's Mail*, is to glue in a piece of thin, tapered hardwood at the base of the float and attach a thinner latex band. Peter Drennan, master float maker, made me some simple peacock quill lift floats with hard plastic base inserts which I found to be ideal.

In calm conditions and in water of moderate depth, a simple thin antenna float will deal with almost any situation involving bottom feeding tench. Sometimes the regular lift float registers a bite that is too fast to hit. The 'dotted' flat top float often goes under like greased lightning. These kinds of bites, when they come, demand intense concentration and very quick reactions. The thin antenna, because it tends to 'slow down' bites, helps do away with much of the need for speed and helps make tench fishing a more leisurely affair. After all, that's really what we hope for from tench fishing!

The windbeater, with its buoyant sight bulb at the end of its long antenna, has much the same effect. It is an especially good float for night fishing in an illuminated torch beam.

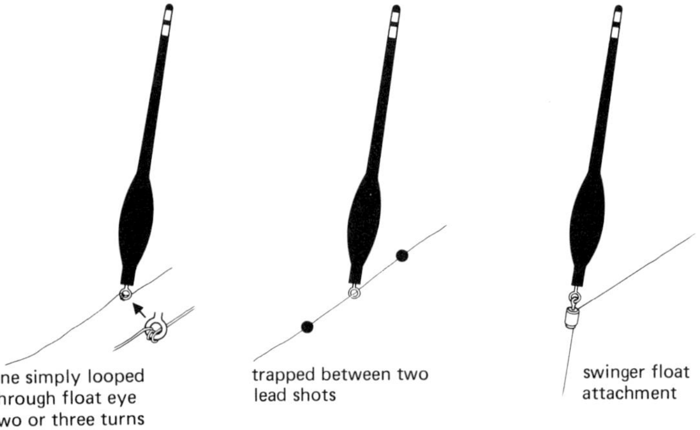


*Figure 9* Three standard ways of attaching a float bottom end only

Polywags, the modern, hard-wearing floats with tough, hardened expanded polystyrene bodies, are extremely useful for long range fishing. They can be attached by a variety of methods at the bottom end only and register bites extremely well. They seem to have replaced the cocktail and missile type floats that once bridged the gap between float fishing and legering. There comes a time, in still water, when the range is too great for comfortable float fishing and the leger must then take over.

Many really large tench have been taken on long range leger tackle and with modern swing, spring and quiver tips employed to register bites, the method should not be overlooked.

Floatless, leadless tackles are also useful at times especially during darkness when tench seem more likely to pick up large baits confidently.

But most tench fishers will agree, I'm sure, that watching a bite on float tackle is the ultimate in tench fishing pleasure. I certainly prefer it to any other style of fishing, and although I do not particularly care for sliding floats, I have learned to appreciate them in deep water situations.

I use almost any kind of bottom buoyancy float, but have found the large sized waggler or polywag to be as good as any. Onions and duckers can also be adapted for the same situation. Attachments and slider knots are shown in figures 9–13.

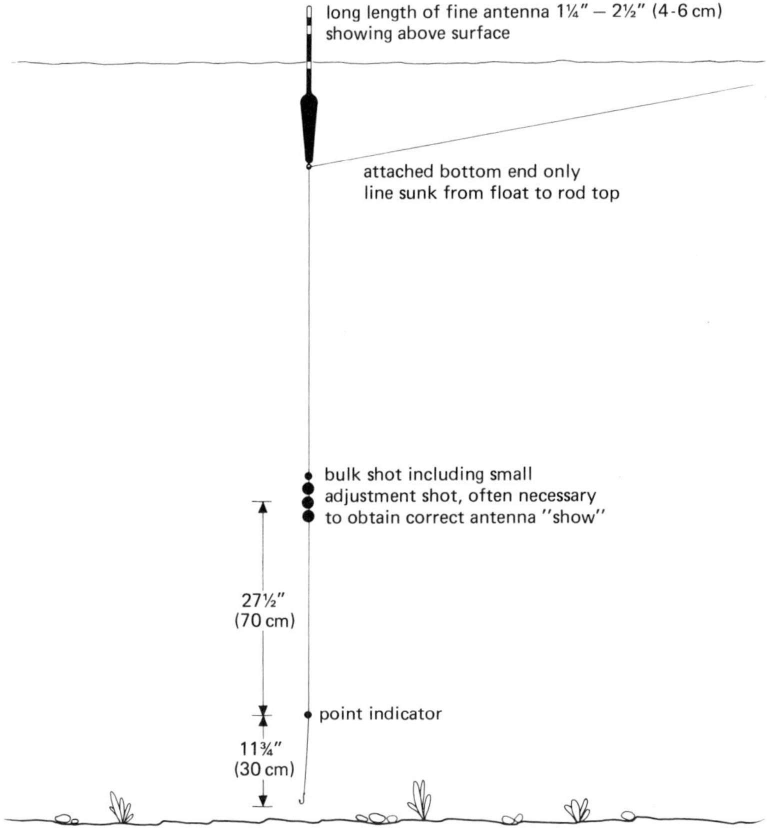


*Figure 10* Antenna float attached bottom end only

Zoomer floats can be used effectively from a boat for casting directly to a margin of reed or rush. The loaded float reaches the edge first, the bait swings under it and comes to rest in the 'danger area'. A simple makeshift float for this kind of fishing was devised by Ken Taylor (figure 14).

Most tench fishing floats then are either straight-stemmed or bottom buoyancy types, but there is a case for a small amount of top buoyancy when it is necessary to allow the bait to drift under the influence of a light breeze. There are times when tench will take

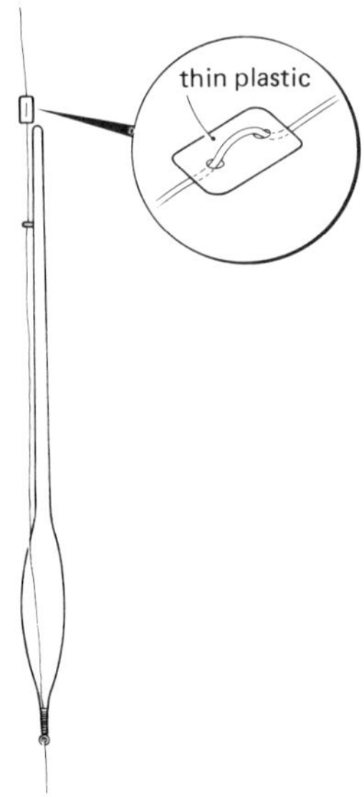


*Figure 11* Plastic stop for use with sliding floats

a bait moving slowly along the bottom, and if a top-buoyancy float is so set that the breeze will drag the bait and – say – one bottom shot *slowly* along the bottom, bites will come often enough to warrant the change. This idea will *not* normally work in a strong wind.

Float fishing in still water for tench, using small baits, can be a fairly critical business and it is essential for floats to be consistent. There was a time when I made most of my own floats, and I still find some pleasure in fashioning them from goose, turkey and swan quills, simply because I *like* feather floats and enjoy using those natural materials. I still make the odd few just for fun but I usually give my creations away to the kids nearby. The reason, of course, is that despite my liking for them, I realize that, technically, they are not as good as the modern commercial patterns available today.

I do not have the skill to make those and, if I did, there would be no consistency. When I make a float it's strictly a 'one off' job and there are never two quite the same. For some reason I cannot duplicate and if, as has happened from time to time, I make a float that suits a particular purpose, there's no way I can replace it if I lose it.

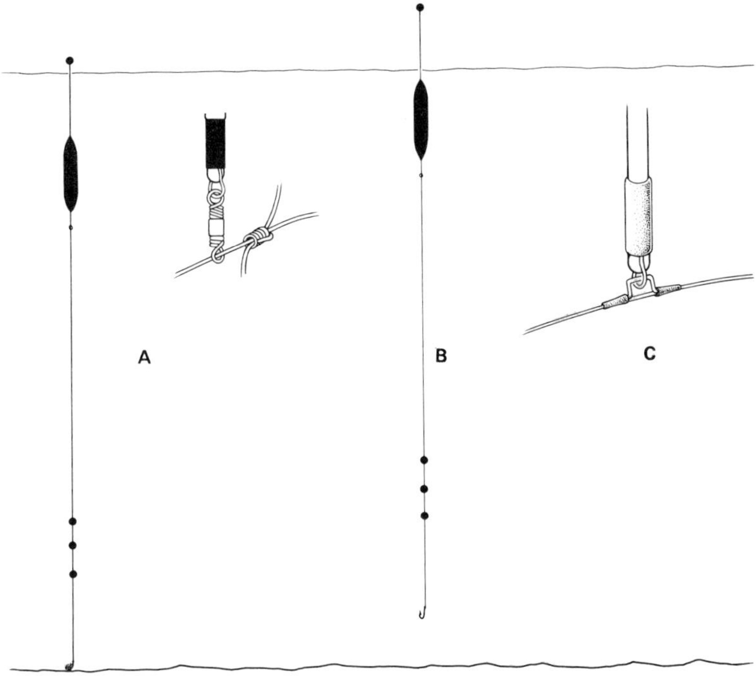


*Figure 12* The beacon float correctly shotted showing a simple slider stop (A and B), and the attachment originally used by Richard Walker (C)

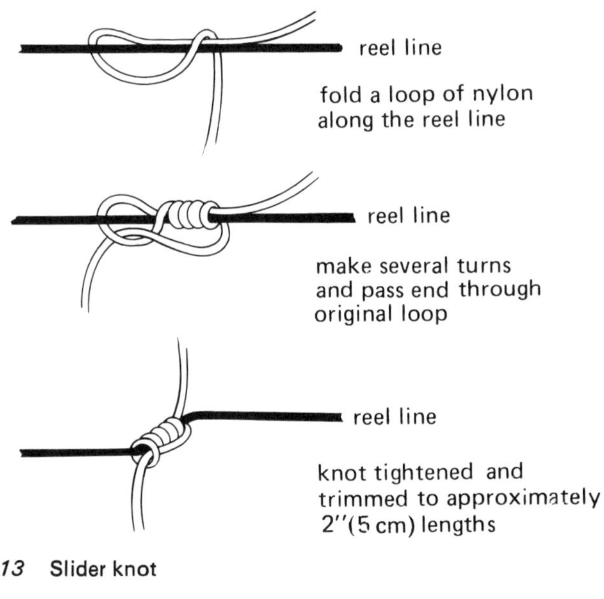


*Figure 13* Slider knot

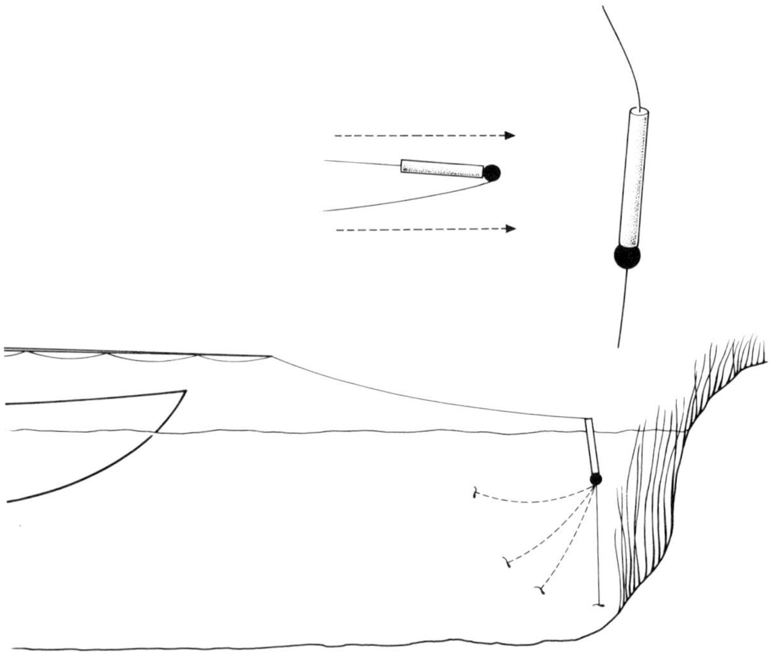

*Figure 14* Makeshift zoomer float devised by Ken Taylor for fishing from a boat close to a margin of reeds or rushes

Modern floats, generally speaking, are, or should be, consistent. If you buy – say – a ducker, flat-top or antenna float of a particular brand, it ought to follow that the next one or the next dozen you buy will be identical regarding shot carrying capacity and behaviour in the water. That's important, when you consider special situations. If you've gone to a certain amount of trouble to get the shotting and bait presentation correct and begin catching fish, you need to be able to duplicate that set-up entirely in the event of float loss or breakage. If you have another, identical float to hand you can be back in business pretty quickly; if not you have to re-think the situation out with another pattern in mind. It's not impossible, of course, but it *does* waste valuable fishing time.

Where long periods between bites are expected, the situation is, perhaps, not so critical and some of the floats I've been playing around with recently have not taken these extreme circumstances into account. So far I've only made three of them and unless I take out a second mortgage or something equally desperate, I doubt if I'll make many more! They're still-water floats with high-powered beta lights in the tips, and although I have used them many times I realize that there is still room for improvement.

Luminous floats are not new. Wasn't it old Isaac himself who told of using an imprisoned glow-worm to register bites at night? (Don't shoot me down if it wasn't – but *someone* did!)

Luminous paint, luminous tape and lower-powered beta lights have all been put to use for after-dark float-fishing, and while there was nothing basically wrong with the idea, these creations were restricted to short range work because they simply were not visible much more than a rod's length away. For near-bank work they showed up well enough but, because they were viewed from above, they tended to remain visible even when pulled under water. In the darkness, of course, there is no background or structure to relate movement; just an inky blackness that plays tricks with the eyes and conjures up all sorts of imaginary gyrations. You can, if you stare at a blob of luminous material (in or out of the water) for long enough, make yourself believe it's moving when it isn't.

The high-powered beta light floats were the result of experiments by Dick Walker and those I've been using are visible at much longer range. Their effective bite registration is remarkable. At fifteen yards or more they remain visible as long as the tip remains out of the water. The moment it goes under (because of the lowering of the viewing angle) it disappears. Sinks without trace as it were! If a 'lift' bite occurs and pushes the float higher out of the water, the luminous tip is then reflected in the water below and shows up either as an elongated version or, in extreme cases, two distinct glows! It's very fascinating, and, more important, very practical.

I first used them for carp up in Yorkshire and, after seeing the way they behaved, became an immediate convert. You can, without any doubt whatsoever, see *exactly* which way the fish is moving off, and once it has been hooked, you need only watch the float, glowing like a miniature beacon in the darkness, to know where it is within a few feet.

One of the carp I caught on that early opening day would almost certainly have been lost in a jungle of lily roots had I not stopped it in time. As it was I was one jump ahead of it at all times because I could actually *see* the path it was taking by the beta light float. I'd taken the precaution of noting the snags in daylight, of course.

Some of my local fishing friends have seen me using them since and have complimented me for exploiting them, but I take no credit for the idea myself. In fact, when Dick Walker first told me about them I was not in the least interested.

Previous experiences with other luminous floats had not impressed me, but when I saw their true value I immediately 'borrowed' one from his box, and forgot to return it! Since then I've found them invaluable for tench fishing at night.

There is undoubtedly a good case for making and using these floats, and I'm confident that they *will* help still-water night fishers enormously. But there are snags. The lowest powered beta light tube for practical purposes of this kind is one of 420 micro-lamberts, and to make a float incorporating one of these will cost in the region of £4! If you lost it first throw it would be a pretty expensive chuck, so it's wise to take precautions. One simple idea, of course, is to use a reel line stronger than the 'leader' below the float. That way, any breakage should occur below the float and ensure its being retrieved intact. The point of attachment to the line must be a particularly safe one, and it's a matter of personal preference how it's done. I like the bottom-end-only attachment, but I'm aware that it is, perhaps, more vulnerable than regular top-and-bottom attachment.

Another problem exists regarding the fixing of the beta light into the float and, of course, which kind of float to use for best effect. It's not an easy choice, because the beta light tube itself has no spare glass at either end. If you *insert* the tube *into* the top of a quill or hollow antenna you cover up part of its luminosity. If you stick it directly on to the top of a float you risk losing it if the glue is not absolutely reliable. And, of course, there's always the danger of hitting a branch or some other obstruction and causing an impact separation.

Peter Drennan suggested making a small thin wire 'cage' to house the tube and a sino-acrylate adhesive as extra insurance. I've no real experience of modern adhesives except to say that some are not strictly impervious to water, and I suggest that, before taking chances, a bond should be tested for a day or two in a tank of water.

The last tench of a small catch is returned after a long night's beta light float fishing

The thin wire cage idea works well enough and if the whole tip is afterwards dipped in Vycoat and allowed to set, the effect is reasonably safe. I'm not too sure about the visibility of the transparent coating, however, and I think it's possible that this reduces the effective sight range fractionally.

The weight of the beta light tube, plus its little wire cage, plus its extra coating, has a slight effect on the buoyancy of the float's antenna, so it is essential to shot the rig correctly in *daylight*. You can get into all kinds of bother if you leave it until dark. Peter has now come up with yet another idea regarding the float's buoyancy and the possibility of wind submersion. He suggests a small bulb of balsa or polystyrene to improve the tip-buoyancy. I believe this will work and I believe, too, that it will help during that short period between daylight and darkness proper. These luminous float tips *do not* show up well until it is really dark and a suitably coloured buoyant 'bob', immediately below the luminous tip, may very well be the answer to this rather serious drawback; but we won't know until the float has been properly field tested.

Meanwhile, I'm satisfied that the advantages offered are worth the cost involved.

I doubt if any manufacturer would consider making these floats, as they're unlikely to be a worthwhile proposition, so if we want them we'll have to make our own, take our chances, and learn as we go on.

One word of warning. Try not to lose or misplace one of these floats during daylight. If you do, you'll have to go back after dark to find it!

The minor drawbacks are more than compensated for by the advantages these floats have to offer and as glues and transparent tubings improve so will the finished beta light float become a regular item of tench fishing equipment.

We probably will not catch any more tench because of them, but those we do catch will come to net with a lot less trouble, and I am convinced that the beta light float constitutes a major breakthrough in the ever improving float-fishing field. I know my tench fishing has been and will continue to be all the better for them.

# Index

# Fishing for Tench